# John Witherspoon

Portrait of John Witherspoon

# John Witherspoon

## Parson
## Politician
## Patriot

## Martha Lou Lemmon Stohlman

WESTMINSTER/JOHN KNOX PRESS
Louisville, Kentucky

BOOK DESIGN BY DOROTHY E. JONES

Published by Westminster/John Knox Press
Louisville, Kentucky

PRINTED IN THE UNITED STATES OF AMERICA
9  8  7  6  5  4  3  2  1


PHOTO CREDITS: Princeton University Library, Frontispiece and pp. 23, 63, 73, and 168; Elizabeth G. C. Menzies from *Princeton Architecture* (Princeton University Press, 1967), p. 93; The Art Museum, Princeton University, pp. 96–97; Independence National Historical Park Collection, p. 145.

---

**Library of Congress Cataloging-in-Publication Data**

Stohlman, Martha Lou Lemmon.
  John Witherspoon : parson, politician, patriot.

  Bibliography: p.
  1. Witherspoon, John, 1723–1794. 2. Statesmen—United States—Biography. 3. Presbyterian Church—United States—Clergy—Biography. I. Title.
E302.6.W7S76 1989    973.3′092′4 [B]    88-26132
ISBN 0-664-24795-4 (pbk.)

To Janet Harbison Penfield
with admiration, affection, and gratitude

# Contents

# Illustrations

# Preface

Ask an American who John Witherspoon was and his answer will likely be, "I don't know." Ask a Scotsman, in whose land Witherspoon spent most of his life, with a name widely known in the eighteenth century, and the answer is apt to be the same. A few may remember that he was a Presbyterian minister who signed the Declaration of Independence and president of the College of New Jersey, which later became Princeton University. He deserves to be better known.

This articulate, passionate man seemed at home in America from the moment he landed in Philadelphia in 1768. He was a forty-five-year-old parish minister, known as a preacher, writer, and debater, most of whose published works pertained to theological or ecclesiastical subjects. In America he instantly became an educator, both administrative and pedagogic, plunging into plans for grammar school, college, and graduate studies as if he had been a headmaster or principal all of his life. A gifted teacher at all levels, he saw 478 students graduate during his twenty-six years at the college. Many entered high offices in government, church, and education, and they all knew him well.

How have we missed him?

Partially the answer lies in his writing, which is heavy going for post-Hemingway readers. The sermons which comprise more than half his publications often bury truly edifying ideas in qualifications and dependent clauses. His lectures on moral philosophy, divinity, and eloquence are taken from notes which, by his own admission, were not prepared for publication, though they have interest. The essays on a variety of subjects are most approachable.

Partially, the answer lies in the destruction, both deliberate and inadvertent, of his papers. British soldiers destroyed the contents of his office in Nassau Hall, and Witherspoon himself makes his biographers wince at his order late in life to a dutiful wife to burn papers he had preserved at home. Recipients of his letters were negligent, and thus relatively few survive a large correspondence.

The earlier of two existing biographies was published only in 1974. Ashbel Green, Witherspoon's student and then colleague at Princeton, wrote appreciatively and comprehensively—and almost illegibly—of his professor and friend. Green's manuscript, intended to introduce a new edition of Witherspoon's works around 1840, was lost when the project failed. When next heard of, it turned up in 1861 "in the interior of Scotland," where the Reverend Nicholas Murray found it and presented it to the New Jersey Historical Society. It lay in the Society's archives in Newark until the Council of the Society of the Colonial Wars of the State of New Jersey recently commissioned Prof. Henry L. Savage of Princeton to edit it. It is now available in a limited edition.

In 1925, Varnum Lansing Collins' two-volume *President Witherspoon* gave a full and scholarly account of the man, more detailed than the average reader might wish. Out of print for some years, it was reissued in spring 1975. Both of these books are available to scholars but are not likely to make Witherspoon's name a household word in the celebration of our country's bicentennial.

Princeton Theological Seminary has sponsored this book and helped in preparing the manuscript for the printer. My commission from the seminary was to write "a compact, readable account of Witherspoon—something that Presbyterians, both clergy and laity, and Americans with any interest in their history would enjoy." I have taken to the word *enjoy*, which has probably been the ultimate criterion for selection of material. I hope to have given the reader reasons for my admiration of a courageous preacher, never mealymouthed, who was yet tolerant of human foible and gentle enough to have been a sympathetic pastor.

Witherspoon's sermons start with a stern exposition of Christian truth and end with examples from everyday that reveal the preacher's tolerance for man's weakness and inability to reach his ideals. His essays can be acute, detailed, and often humorous observations of daily life. He wrote on parents' pride in supposedly smart sayings of their children, on a young woman's attempt to make learned conversation on the classics with Dr. Witherspoon (who would prefer an honest comment on the weather), on the rejection of some men of a reasonable idea simply because it came from their wives.

Since Collins wrote, only one substantial new source has come to light. Twenty-four letters from Witherspoon to Benjamin Rush emerged in 1943. These, together with other pertinent letters, were published in an engaging volume edited by Lyman Butterfield, *John Witherspoon Comes to America*. Chapter 3 of the present volume is based on that book. A substantial portion of the rest of it derives from Green and Collins or their sources. Summaries of sermons are my own, and I have drawn on articles written since Collins' time on special aspects of Witherspoon or his period.

Prof. Wesley Frank Craven of Princeton University and Prof. Lefferts Loetscher of Princeton Theological Seminary have been good enough to talk with me about Witherspoon and his time and to recommend more sources than I could pursue. Prof. Julian Boyd kindly encouraged this project and gave the reference on Witherspoon as an economist. Prof. John Mulder of Princeton Theological Seminary and Prof. James H. Smylie of Union Seminary, Richmond, Virginia, generously reviewed the manuscript and made valuable suggestions. I am grateful to Mrs. Ario Pardee, present owner and resident of Tusculum, for an attic-to-basement tour of the house that Witherspoon built.

I would be more humble about qualifying as a happy writer if, in working on the book, one thing had not become clear: The English humorist might be right who said, "History is not what you thought. It is what you can remember." What is better remembered than what is enjoyed?

M.L.L.S.

# 1

# A Fighter Is Born

### . . . great heats and divisions

*—Principal George Hill, St. Mary's College*
*University of St. Andrews*

## 1723–1757

"Cousin America has eloped with a Presbyterian parson,"
Horace Walpole wrote in 1775. Walpole did not designate
the parson, but the image might have fit John Witherspoon.
American history books make slight mention of Witherspoon, yet his enemies considered him a firebrand of the
Revolution. British soldiers burned his effigy. John Adams
met him in 1774, only six years after his arrival from Scotland, and he found Witherspoon "as hearty a Friend as any
of the Natives—an animated Son of Liberty."

Witherspoon had left a church in Paisley, where more
than a thousand heard him regularly on Sunday morning—
and afternoon. In Princeton he would amiably greet a class,
"How do ye do, lads?" and the lads, with one of his Gaelic
words, would answer, "Braly, sir, braly"—very well, sir. In
lecturing to them, he avoided abstractions. If the subject
was civil liberty, for example, he simply claimed its value for
"its tendency to put all the human powers into motion."

He was a direct, practical, winsome, at times formidable
man. Ashbel Green wrote that only Washington had more
of "the quality called *presence*—a quality powerfully felt but

not to be described." Moses Coit Tyler wrote that he came "at the right moment to the right spot, in the right way."

How did it happen that a beloved Scottish pastor could be lured to the colonies and so quickly involved in its struggle for independence? Already he was known as a parson of distinction and influence. Interestingly enough, his preparation to be also a politician and a patriot was begun in the Church of Scotland.

Eighteenth-century Scotland was an animated country, small enough for its intellectuals to know and stimulate one another. John Witherspoon had the good fortune to be born in 1723, contemporary and countryman of Adam Smith, Tobias Smollett, Francis Hutcheson, David Hume, and many other keen Scotsmen. Adam Smith was proposing that a person knows what is best for him, will do what he must to satisfy his need—and a good thing too! Rousseau was saying that children should grow and learn, motivated by wish, unburdened by a sense of duty. The emphasis upon intuition, nature, and feeling as guides to action came to many as an exciting revelation, to others as a clear sign of spiritual decay. What became of duty? Could one ignore imperatives of Scripture? He who knows Scottish Presbyterians can guess the source of those questions.

Scottish Presbyterians did not, however, fall into one camp. They too took sides. The orthodox were referred to, surprisingly, as Popular; liberals were called Moderate. Moderates found poetry, drama, and literature engaging vehicles of religious expression. They passed lightly over the concept of sinful man and his relationship to God. They seized upon the freedom of every man to interpret the Bible for himself and dismayed many by caring more for graceful expression in sermons than for content.

The Popularists, however, protested the ignoring of fundamentals of Christianity, with its consequent slackness in personal conduct and a flabby evangelism, if any at all. Not opposing literature per se, they sought their truth in the sterner admonitions of Scripture and in revelation arising from serious personal devotion. For them, deeper religious meaning certainly did not emerge from sheer pleasure.

This division still looms in the sober search of inquiring Christian minds. One answer or the other is often in the ascendant in different eras or among different people. These strongly felt opposing perspectives are always stimulating for a young minister with conviction and a gift for words. The youthful John Witherspoon was willingly drawn into the fray. He framed his own thoughts vividly. He accrued followers until he became the recognized leader of his party and inspired sufficient hostility to testify to his importance. The climate was right to nourish the good preacher, teacher, and political man that Witherspoon was to become.

John's education had started with his mother's teaching. In the tiny village of Gifford in the rolling countryside fourteen miles east of Edinburgh, Anna Walker Witherspoon early introduced her son to the printed word. At four John read from the Bible and eventually could recite a great part of the New Testament and much of Watts's *Psalms and Hymns.*

John's father, James Witherspoon, was minister of Yester parish, and the kind of man he was depends upon whom you read. John's schoolmate in Edinburgh, Alexander Carlyle, who more than once visited the family, makes dreadful allusions to a father who was "sulky and tyrannical, . . . given to gluttony, . . . and fat as a porpoise." Nor did he think much of "the depth of his reading, . . . [only] the sermons of the French Calvinist ministers." He does admit that the Reverend James Witherspoon "was not without parts, if the soul had not been buried under a mountain of flesh." James may have been given to overeating, but it is unlikely that without real capability he would have served on so many committees in General Assembly or have been the royal chaplain who preached before the lord high commissioner. John's father and his eminent uncle Thomas Walker, also a clergyman, are credited by Ashbel Green with considerable

influence on the boy's character and style. At one catas-
trophic time in his early ministry, John attributed to his
father's encouragement his ability to continue as a
preacher.

His mother's ancestry traces through a solid line of clergymen, extending back to John Knox himself. Concerning
the lady herself, we know only that she bore six children,
that one of her sons was lost in the West Indies, and that
a daughter who married a schoolmaster in Edinburgh was
mother of a tutor to Sir Walter Scott.

The grammar school at Haddington, four miles from
Gifford, was the scene of young John's first formal education as it had been for John Knox. So well did he do in his
studies of English, the classics, and mathematics that at
thirteen he was ready for the university in Edinburgh. He
once said that at that time he knew Latin, Greek, and French
"as well as he ever did."

We cannot know how his parents felt about sending a
thirteen-year-old son into the city alone, but the situation
was not then uncommon. There were even younger students. And the university itself, when John enrolled on
November 1, 1735, was not, after all, New York University.

John, feeling his responsibility as the oldest son, was a
sober student. Not so his housemate, Alexander Carlyle,
who was a bounding extrovert given to dancing and bil-
liards. He could scarcely have been more different from the
careful and conscientious John, whom he describes as "a
good scholar, far advanced for his age, very sensible and
shrewd." Otherwise Carlyle's memories of John, recorded
in 1800 in his autobiography, were no mellower than his
memories of John's father. He pictures his schoolmate as a
traditionally shy and awkward country boy who dazzled no
one. Besides being bad tempered and speaking in a flat,
unpleasant voice, he was "close, and suspicious, and jeal-
ous, and always aspiring to a superiority that he was not able
to maintain." Carlyle is a real gift to a biographer of the
antihero school.

In the Edinburgh house where John and Alexander had rooms four other students and a tutor each afternoon prepared lessons. Lectures were in old houses described as "low and ruinous," and Carlyle records this schedule of Prof. John Stevenson: 8 A.M., Aristotle; 11 A.M., Locke; 2 P.M., ancient philosophers—with examinations on each three times a week. For both young men Stevenson was their outstanding teacher—civil, kind, and enlarging their minds, according to Carlyle; evoking a love for literature and respect for style, form, and the English language itself, according to Witherspoon. Interestingly enough, at that time English was only a written language in Scotland. In America, Witherspoon's accent and vocabulary were to give trouble at times to his listeners.

The boys were fortunate in having at least one absorbing teacher, for their own coterie and whatever classes it chose to attend composed almost their total relation to the university. Professors gave lectures on a take-it-or-leave-it basis, with no registrar to check credits. Students attended the classes they wanted, stayed as long as their fathers would finance them, and often left without a degree. Only three were granted in 1749.

Into three years John pressed the usual four years' work for the Master of Arts degree—in the apparent absence then of a Bachelor of Arts degree—with classes in Latin, mathematics, natural philosophy (science), and moral philosophy. Toward the end of 1738, with four other students he petitioned the principal to permit them to publish theses and to defend them publicly. Thus, just after his sixteenth birthday in February 1739, John became a Master of Arts with a thesis written in Latin, *De Mentis Immortalitate,* signed Joannes Wederspan.

On holidays, Carlyle and Witherspoon seemed congenial enough. They visited each other's home, enjoying the fishing at Gifford and jolly evenings with young relatives and friends. Alexander commented on John's lively interest in young ladies, especially at the Carlyles' in Prestonpans, where there were many—and "no restraint from an austere father." Whatever the reveling amounted to, it led the old Carlyle to write, "I always considered the austerity of manners and aversion to social joy which he affected afterwards as the arts of hypocrisy and ambition."

Possibly this was a touch of sour grapes. Carlyle confessed that, for all the charms he undoubtedly possessed, he was refused by the first two ladies he proposed to and did not marry until much later. John, however, was happily married at twenty-five and, widowed in old age, retained sufficient attraction to win a bride of twenty-four. He too had a youthful disappointment during student years from a Miss Annie Hogg. She never wed but remained his faithful correspondent until his death, sending to America most of the personal news that reached him from Scotland.

John and Alexander, whatever their diversities, continued together as students through seven years. Carlyle must have found something agreeable in his companion. Although for years the two met at General Assemblies, the autobiographer mentions John only in his student days and concludes with the ambiguous statement: "The future life and public character of Dr. Witherspoon is perfectly known." He is silent on the great literary duel between them, known to everyone in the Church of Scotland.

The men drifted apart on opposite edges of the widening rift between the Popular party, which John led, and the Moderates, of whom Carlyle was a perfect representative. Well known among the literati, Carlyle was a friend of David Garrick and Tobias Smollett, and Sir Walter Scott was struck by his appearance to the point of writing: "The grandest demigod I ever saw was Dr. Carlyle, . . . commonly called *Jupiter Carlyle* from having sat more than once [for a painter] for the king of the gods and men."

John was only twenty when he became a doctor of theology and his home presbytery of Haddington licensed him as a preacher. For two years no church sought the services of the youthful minister. He was then invited to preach in

competition for the living at Beith, an attractive village in
Ayrshire. John was chosen from the four candidates, having
thus passed what was known as "the first trial." "The second trial" was a two-day examination by presbytery during
which members of the congregation could submit written
complaints known as "libels" should they know of doctrinal
unsoundness or moral turpitude in the candidate. His thesis
was questioned, and he was called upon to defend it. He
satisfied his listeners and was ordained on April 11, 1745.
His annual salary was £17 12s. 6d., plus 79 bolls of meal and
a 31-acre glebe. Webster defines a boll as "four Winchester
bushels" or "about 2–6 bushels in present measures," and
it varies when applied to wheat or oats. So much for equiva-
lents.

In the calling of a minister another sharp rock in the
stream of Scottish Presbyterianism is revealed. The Moderates favored the choice by patrons, usually the local noblemen, although the Church of Scotland had ruled that congregations must have a voice in selection. The
proportionate influence of patron and parish was a vexed
question for centuries and provoked "great heats and divisions," according to Professor Hill, who wrote a history of
it.

The Popularists wanted congregations to find a minister
congenial to their needs and temper. On occasion, churches
had refused candidates whom bullheaded patrons named
even though they were inaudible in the pulpit, unable to
speak to Gaelic congregations, were Dissenters, or even
were downright ignorant of theology. In the face of church
law, patronage long remained a source of distress. The
Popularists deplored the Moderates' preference for "literary infidels" and their hostility "to every effort in favor of
orthodoxy of doctrine and strictness of discipline."

Once settled at Beith, the young pastor had a year to
accustom himself to his new life before he suffered an unforeseen experience. Bonnie Prince Charlie arrived from
France in 1745. This led to elevated hopes in some quarters

that once again a Stuart might rule Scotland. After his success at Prestonpans and an invasion and retreat from England, his army was about to clash once more, early in 1746, with the British. In Beith, there was no lengthy pondering of relative roles of church and state nor of hawks and doves. The congregation prayerfully decided, along with most Lowlanders, to support England and the Duke of Cumberland against rebelling Highlanders. It raised money and sent off its young minister at the head of 150 militiamen to join the royal forces at Stirling.

They were some twenty miles on their way when military officers in Glasgow, quickly assessing the untrained group, decided that His Majesty's army could win without it. The company was dismissed. But Witherspoon and his beadle, "bearing a trusty sword, still preserved and dearly prized by that gentleman's descendants," according to Collins, went on to watch the unexpected defeat on January 17 of the royal forces at Falkirk. Nonparticipants though they were, the beadle's conspicuous sword convicted them in the eyes of the Young Pretender's men, who took them prisoner.

For a week the two were moved about with the rebels before being confined with fifteen other loyalists in Castle Doune near Stirling. One of these, John Home, had been in the university with Witherspoon and was to be another of his dramatic Moderate antagonists. Even sharing a prison did not unite them. Home joined an escape group, while Witherspoon decided against it—wisely, it seems, since one captive fell from the blanket rope to a severe injury and the next one fell to his death. But John and his beadle were released and returned to Beith after less than a month's absence.

At about this time he began to have "a sudden and overwhelming presentiment in the midst of a service that he would not live to finish." For three years he was haunted by the clutch of this unreasoning dread, but firm and gentle urging from his father kept him at his work. The therapy that succeeded for him was perhaps what he used years later

The church at Beith, Scotland, Witherspoon's first pastorate

when his friend Ashbel Green suffered a similar affliction. Young Green, convinced of impending failure, was about to refuse a call from Philadelphia when Witherspoon said to him: "Go you down to Philadelphia, and do as well as you can, and God will help you. Take everything with *moderation.* . . . Do everything just as if you were *well,* and after a while *you will be so."* It worked.

As for Witherspoon, he suffered throughout his life from insomnia and hypersensitivity to sound and smell. He said that he had deliberately to restrain himself from passionate discussion or oratory that might engender high feeling lest his emotions get out of hand. His manner of speaking, often phlegmatic, may have stemmed from this voluntary restraint. The cause of his affliction, which later affected him at times, is uncertain. He told Green, without elaborating, that a great ordeal had befallen him at Beith. Was it the military excursion? Probably not. His brush with war was brief and peripheral, and later, as an American patriot, he showed no aversion to war on principle nor, apparently, perturbation from actual proximity of enemy armies.

After two years in Beith, he married a resident of the vicinity, Elizabeth Montgomery of Craighouse, who was two years his senior. In the next eight years they led a full life together, with hours of gold and hours of lead. Elizabeth bore five children, two of whom died, a daughter at six and a little son who celebrated only one birthday. John's days saw him tending parish duties, riding horseback, fishing, golfing, and gaining quite a reputation at curling. In the evenings there was plenty to read and to write about.

Those years when he was stuck away in a small village, his rereading of the minutes of judicatories and pamphlets gave food for thought. John liked to write, and one of his articles, published in the *Scots Magazine* in 1753, was forwarded to America. Thus his support of Common Sense philosophy preceded him to the land he was to adopt. John's lively mind and dynamic partisanship drove him to pen two works that made him well known throughout Scot-

land: a satire on the Moderates called *Ecclesiastical Characteristics* in 1753 and his *Essay on Justification* in 1756.

*Ecclesiastical Characteristics* is not the title one would
choose for a best seller, but this sixty-page pamphlet became one. In seven editions and nine reprints it reached
England, Holland, and eventually America, as well as Scotland. Some rated its author's acerbic ridicule of the Moderates in a class with Swift. It was unsigned and for many years
unacknowledged by Witherspoon, but from the first its au-
thorship was suspected. The 100,000 Moderates outnumbered the orthodox and controlled some 1,200 churches in
Scotland by 1765. It is worthwhile to see how these dissenters appeared to their formidable adversary John Witherspoon, who turned upon them their favorite maxim of
Shaftesbury's: "Ridicule is the test of truth."

The pamphlet contained thirteen maxims for "a Plain
and Easy way to attaining to the character of a Moderate
Man." He emerges as an intellectual, well read in current
literature, pleased with himself for belonging to a self-
protecting, cliquish group who feels decidedly superior to
old-fashioned quoters of Scripture, affably tolerant of
"good humoured vices," proud to be selected as a pastor
by noble patrons, and caring nothing for what the congregation—poor ignorants—might think of him. Convinced
that the best thing to be said of a man is that he has "a warm
and good heart," he would consider orthodox churchmen
knaves and fools. He would "never speak of the Confession
of Faith but with a sneer" and would "drop sly hints that he
does not thoroughly believe it"; if truth were known, he
would feel "utter abhorrence at the vile hedge of distinction, the Confession of Faith."

Maxim VI requires that the Moderate be contemptuous
"of all kinds of learning but one, which is to understand
Leibniz's scheme." Here Witherspoon bursts into an
"Athenian Creed" for the Moderate who has mastered
Leibniz. This is such an excellent example of the author's
style and so well epitomizes his message that no biographer

can resist it. The antitheses to Christianity that Witherspoon perceived in the Moderates' philosophy stick out of
the creed like quills on a porcupine:

> I believe in the beauty and comely proportions of Dame Nature,
> and graciously obliged (blessed be its name) to make us all very
> good.

> I believe that the universe is a huge machine, wound up from
> everlasting by necessity, and consisting of an indefinite number
> of links and chains, each in a progressive motion towards the
> zenith of perfection, and meridian of glory; that I myself am a
> little glorious piece of clockwork, a wheel within a wheel, or
> rather a pendulum in this grand machine, swinging hither and
> thither by the different impulses of fate and destiny; that my
> soul (if I have any) is an imperceptible bundle of exceeding
> minute corpuscles, much smaller than the finest Holland sand;
> and that certain persons in a very eminent station are nothing
> else but a huge collection of necessary agents, who can do
> nothing at all.

> I believe that there is no ill in the universe, nor any such thing
> as virtue absolutely considered; that those things vulgarly
> called sins, are only errors in the judgment, and foils to set off
> the beauty of Nature, or patches to adorn her face; that the
> whole race of intelligent beings, even the devils themselves (if
> there are any) shall finally be happy; so that Judas Iscariot is by
> this time a glorified saint, and it is good for him that he hath
> been born.

> In fine, I believe in the divinity of L.S——[Lord Shaftesbury],
> the saintship of Marcus Antoninus, the perspicuity and sub-
> limity of A——e [Le Père Yves André], and the perpetual
> duration of Mr. H——n's [Francis Hutcheson's] works not-
> withstanding their present tendency to oblivion. Amen.

Thus did Witherspoon hold a mirror before the face of
the Moderate man. In effect he said, If you refuse to take
seriously a Christian creed, here is your alternative. Moderate men reacted instantly and vociferously, maligning in
strong words "a man unfit to be a member of any peaceable

society." This went on for years. We may imagine that each new printing added more new defensive Moderates, while the assenting orthodox nodded heads with satisfaction.

The *Essay on Justification* was not such a bombshell. In fact, one is tempted to conclude that this essay proves how right Witherspoon was when, in defending the *Ecclesiastical Characteristics*, he saw a greater vividness and revelation in satire than in straight exposition. However, what seems to us verbose struck his contemporaries in a more leisurely age as sound development of an argument with plenty of time to digest the words. At least, the essay was widely read in its three editions, with extra printings later. It was an amplification of two sermons, running to about sixty pages. It is a good example of John's theology. It gains some of its points by setting off the orthodox belief against Moderate interpretations.

Its message is: *What you believe determines what you do.* The writer cannot hold with a current notion "that it is a small matter what a man believe, if his life be good," for, he asserts, it is surely "a foolish and unreasonable supposition that a man may believe wrong and yet lead as good a life as he that believes right."

According to Witherspoon, the Christian who accepts the notion that man is by nature in "a lost condemned state" standing in the need of "pardon through the righteousness and renovation by the Spirit of Christ" cannot be an arrogant man, thinking of himself as self-made. Further, to recognize his dependence upon God is wonderfully encouraging, and to know strength available from beyond himself is a powerful motive to action. It gives a man "the strongest influence in animating . . . [his] own endeavors." Witherspoon urges us to look at the behavior of people: "Do not all careless, profane, and sensual livers, almost to a man, profess themselves enemies to this doctrine?" And are not those who "deny their own rightness . . . ordinarily the most tender and fearful of sinning themselves, and the most diligent in promoting the reformation of others"?

John once told a friend that his own belief in the doctrine
of grace rested upon his observation of people who accepted it. Their actions differed markedly from "the un-
tender behavior" of those who did not.

Naturally, he found David Hume's enumeration of virtues "an insult upon reason itself." Hume included "wit,
genius, health, taper [*sic*] legs and broad shoulders among
his virtues." John, though, is leery of too much talent which
is as apt as not "to intoxicate the mind and lead to pride,
arrogance and self-conceit." Likewise, "the master prejudice of this age, viz., 'the innocence of error,' " must be
anathema to the Christian whose belief is that man must
recognize and admit error, then *decide* to accept the grace
of God, freely offered though it be.

Another target of the *Essay* was the preacher who feared
lest preaching on the abundance of God's grace lead to
licentiousness. The question is still with us, as framed suc-
cinctly by W. H. Auden: "Every crook will argue: 'I like
committing crimes. God likes forgiving them. Really the
world is admirably arranged.' " To this, Witherspoon
would be quick to reply, "Yes, and the minute anyone said
such a thing, you would know what kind of person he is,
wouldn't you?"

These and other publications of the young minister, together with his well-thought-out statements firmly expressed at meetings of the judicatories, raised animosity
from Moderates but led the orthodox to recognize a leader.
He was strong, courageous, and adept in extricating himself
from a difficult situation. Ashbel Green takes note also of
"his accurate acquaintance with forms, usages, and prece-
dents in ecclesiastical proceedings, his knowledge of human
nature, and almost intuitive insight into the real merits and
bearing of a litigated question, and his tact and readiness in
managing every cause of which he became the advocate."

Not unexpectedly, when the pulpit became vacant in the
Laigh Kirk at Paisley, a town of twelve thousand some fourteen miles northeast of Beith, the church called John With-

erspoon. In this case, no nobleman but the magistrates and town council were "patrons of the living." With the borough citizens and the session of the church concurring, they chose him in June 1756. It took exactly one year to get him. What followed was doubtlessly done decently and in order, but the procedure was as complicated as a chess game.

The call contained an error and had to be returned to Paisley for correction. Then the Presbytery of Paisley, two months after the initial decision, refused, as Presbyterians say, to grant the call—no reason offered. Inquiry revealed that the *Ecclesiastical Characteristics* had been too much. Even some of the Popular party agreed when Moderates said that no truly Christian man could have been so harsh. The court of appeal in such an instance was the next higher judicatory, the Synod of Glasgow and Ayr. Both presbyteries agreeing, Witherspoon appeared before the synod to speak for himself.

It was a tricky situation. He had not signed the *Characteristics*, nor had he admitted to being its author. In the face of general assumption that he was the writer, to deny it would put him in the position of being a great deceiver for having lived the lie so long. If he admitted it, then he was liable for slandering fellow ministers and stood in danger of actually being turned out of the ministry. He walked this tightwire "with such admirable skill," says Green, "as not merely to obtain a formal acquittal, but to load his prosecutors with the opprobrium of a most unjust, insidious, and inquisitorial proceeding; and this without either admitting or denying that he was the author of the *Characteristics.*"

John had already written *A Serious Apology for the Ecclesiastical Characteristics* by The True Author of the Same. In pleading his case he could use the points in it and, if challenged, could simply claim agreement with a published work whose author was unknown. Everyone in the room knew full well that he *had* written both pieces.

His argument ran that the characteristics described—by

whatever author—were highly visible among Scottish
clergy. Who could deny it? Witherspoon told the synod
meeting that it was "a melancholy truth . . . that irreligion
and infidelity have made a rapid progress among us for
some time." He firmly stated that "unpardoned sin will
never let us rest" and that to be pardoned, sin must be
brought out and confessed. As for the bitter complaint that
ridicule was a wicked weapon, quite unchristian, he countered: Churchmen have always used satire, good men such
as Pascal, Jerome, and Augustine. And what about Elijah?
What about Isaiah? What about Jesus? It is an effective tool.
He suspected that the satirical *Characteristics* had twenty
times more readers than the straightforward *Apology*.

From what we can know today of John's character, we can
see him delivering these remarks not to triumph over others
but with a genuine concern for the health of his church. It
is almost certain that John's own person and sincerity won
the day for him. Otherwise he would have sounded unbear-
ably smug in his further defense of the uses of satire: The
men aimed at in the *Characteristics* have a pride that has
made them dead to advice. There is really, he said, "no
getting at them till their pride is leveled a little by this
dismaying weapon," and, quoting Tertullian, he judges that
"if one can use it with delicacy it is a duty to do so." The
targets of John's dismaying weapon may well have roared
disagreement that "delicacy" could be connected with this
onslaught, but his words sank into his listeners.

In conclusion he pointed out that the laity had not found
the message of the *Characteristics* unjust. He felt that the
church's chief trouble arose from denying to congregations
the right to choose their own clergy and that "the political
measures which have been carrying on for . . . thirty years
. . . in the church of Scotland appear to be ruinous to the
interests of religion." And then dropping the attack, he
eased the way for some listeners to come over to his side.
He hoped, he said, to open the eyes of the many good men
who had reluctantly followed along with common practices.

"The train of circumstances, not always in our own power, sometimes leads good men themselves to support the most corrupt part of a church in their public measures. The boundaries of prudence and zeal are not easily fixed." He ended by beseeching "all convinced that the state of the church of Scotland is such as I have represented, to exert themselves . . . for her preservation and recovery."

This temperate appeal won the day. The synod in December 1756 directed the Presbytery of Paisley to moderate the call. But another half year passed before the path to Paisley was actually cleared.

In this interval John's pen was not idle, and his name became even better known—and worse received if one were not orthodox. His next article appeared in the midst of a horrendous conflict that tore the hearts and minds of all Scotland. The fact that this gigantic battle took place largely on paper does not mean that adrenalin did not flow, tears were not shed, jobs not lost, words not shouted, and friendships not broken forever. Carlyle's mean words about the Witherspoons were written well after this great contention. They likely took on their dark hue from the fact that a focal engagement in the campaign was between Carlyle and Witherspoon.

The issue was: May Christians rightfully attend the theater? The precipitant cause was a play—written by a *clergyman!*—presented in Edinburgh. The padre with the luckless imagination to set down a drama in verse was John Home, Witherspoon's fellow student at Edinburgh and fellow prisoner at Castle Doune. The play was called *Douglas,* and it is devilishly difficult for a reader in the twentieth century to understand its detonating power.

It evidently succeeded in evoking all the cathartic feeling that Aristotle applauded in well-wrought tragedy. Jupiter Carlyle wrote that "the town in general was in an uproar of exultation that a Scotsman had written a tragedy of the first rate, . . . the sentiment of the whole republic of belles-lettres." If the audience could merely have gone home from the performance with whatever internal reverberations stirring drama may produce, all would have been well. But this play was set on a greater stage. It was one act in the drama of Moderates *versus* Popularists. It sounded off thunderous reactions to the questions: Should a minister write a play—ever? Should a Christian go to the theater—to *any* play? If not, why not? These questions were answered in the negative and in the affirmative by sermons, essays, articles, satiric verse, and doggerel, signed and unsigned.

One bore the name of John Witherspoon, a salvo from Beith from the Big Bertha of the Popularist artillery. His *Serious Enquiry into the Nature and Effects of the Stage* asked "Whether supporting and encouraging stage plays, by writing, acting, or attending them, is consistent, or inconsistent, with the character of a Christian." Could plays aid a Christian in his chief purpose: to "aim at the glory of God"?

"The truth is," he wrote, "the need of amusement is much less than people commonly apprehend, and where it is not necessary, it must be sinful." The theater is expensive, both to maintain and to attend. Is it worth it? Are the emotional expenditures attached to it truly recreative? Many characters in plays are not good: they elicit no positive experience and send a viewer away with nothing to strengthen his role as a self-denying Christian. Worse, they have pernicious consequences on those who are "in most danger of infection," those who attend all plays indiscriminately. Strong characters who may themselves be uncorrupted set an example merely by being seen in the theater. In response to the proposition that drama is educational, he asks why "the world or anything else need be known" unless it leads to our spiritual improvement. His opinion that "no woman . . . who has been ten times in a playhouse durst repeat in company all that she has heard there" is, even today, not utterly unthinkable. And should anyone ask, the author explains that his knowledge of the theater is not firsthand but derives from his reading.

Carlyle, a minister himself, was called to reckon with his

presbytery, synod, and finally the General Assembly for "conversing in a familiar manner" with actors and "attending publicly an unlicensed theater." He blusteringly confided to his diary that he "stood up to their fanatical exertion of power which would have kept the younger clergy for half a century longer in the trammels of bigotry . . . and debarred every generous spirit from entering into orders."

The commotion continued for years and perhaps lives on in our own questioning of the effects of television on the crime rate, of modern drama and literature on social behavior. Today the arguments against such influences run more to practical consequences than to moral principles. Not many are asking what Carlyle meant by a "generous spirit," nor whether John was justified in claiming that association with the theater "is inconsistent with the character of a Christian," nor whether, simply, the theater "aims at the glory of God." For those who feel today that learning— from almost any source—of the world's rude ways may enable us to become wise as serpents, there are as many who, as Witherspoon, would ask if those glued to tube and stage are not taking another bite from the apple.

John had one last ecclesiastical altercation while treading water at Beith, waiting for the new call to be cleared. At General Assembly in May he called for the rejection from office of certain elders who had failed to observe the Sabbath and to conduct family worship. By then the Moderates had a number of lawyers on their sessions who also attended Assembly, with their legal vocabulary and manners. Although the lapse that John charged did indeed violate the Patronage Act, the lawyers triumphed over his little band of eight. However, the Popularists soon learned to match them in kind. The litigation that John had long practiced in Scottish judicatories made him wholly at ease in the verbal give-and-take which, in a different context, later became an important part of his life.

At last in June 1757 all requirements to call the new

minister to the Laigh Kirk had been met. John and Elizabeth, with seven-year-old Ann, five-year-old James, and the baby, Barbara, just born in February, moved with their household goods the fourteen miles into Paisley.

# 2

## The Preacher of Paisley

These that have turned
the world upside down
are come hither also.

*Acts 17:6*

### 1757–1768

Gauze Street in Paisley is a reminder that in the eighteenth
century the town was noted for its silk gauzes. The shawls
that bore its name with their paramecium-shaped Indian
pattern are still called Paisley. The textile mills of the nineteenth century have given way to the Coats and Clark spin-
ning mills which today make Paisley the world's largest
thread producer.

The city centers around an abbey that evolved from a
twelfth-century Cluniac priory situated on the rippling
White Cart River. A classical town hall of the nineteenth
century shares the open space around the abbey. High
Street curves upward from it through the business district
to a classical museum building. Here one may see a print of
the small town set in pastoral hills as it was when the Witherspoons arrived. Between 1733 and 1783 Paisley turned
from an unprepossessing village into a thriving little city
well known as a center of weaving.

More than a century ago Paisley was referred to as "the
most intellectual community in Scotland," "a hot bed of the
most advanced political views," a town where "every weaver

is a politician." Perhaps The Reverend Mr. Witherspoon and the weavers' town had a reciprocal effect in motivating each other to intellectual and political exertions. The minister may also have had his influence in a realm noted by the General Assembly. In 1784—admittedly some years after his departure—it received a report that "the oversight of morals in Paisley is unsurpassed in any town of its size in Scotland."

The prosperity of the town at that time is evidenced in salaries of the ministers of the High Church in the abbey and in the Laigh Kirk. Each received £100 per annum, a good £30 above the average pastor's income. It seems small enough, considering that the thirteen hundred persons who often filled the church when John preached presented manifold pastoral obligations too.

The Witherspoons lived in Paisley for ten years. Our sole knowledge of the family in that period is written on tombstones: son George, born in 1762, lived only four months; another son, the last of Elizabeth's ten children, was stillborn in June of the next year, less than two months before little Barbara died at the age of seven. A daughter, Frances, and a son, David, were born in Paisley. Those two, of the five children who grew to adulthood, ended their days in America, in North Carolina.

The public life of the head of the family, however, is preserved in archives and libraries. In the absence of national elections such as ours, the spokesmen for Popularists and Moderates were, in effect, the politicians of the day. W. S. Gilbert's engaging song captures the adjectives that describe us in both our political and religious convictions: "Every boy and every gal / That's born into the world alive / Is either a little Liberal / Or a little Conservative." The conflicts between Popularists and Moderates did not flicker across television screens and evaporate. Those debates flowed into print in the form of essays and sermons to satisfy a large and interested reading public.

A great fraction of John Witherspoon's published work

stems from this period. It consistently reveals two concerns: an engrossing interest and participation in church disputes, and an impassioned and articulate conservative Christian theology.

Consider first his involvement in the organizational machinery of his church. After the ruckus attendant upon his call to Paisley, the Synod of Glasgow and Ayr rather surprisingly elected him moderator the very next year. By May of 1758 he was deep in litigation over a request to make two different sessions for Paisley's High Church and Low Church—his own Laigh Kirk. The very description of the suit as a "Case of the Magistrates and Town-Council of Paisley, the Minister and Session of the Low Church, and the Minister of the High Church of that Town, Appellants, the Reverend the Presbytery of Paisley, respondents at the Bar of the Venerable Assembly" manifests the kind of legal proceedings in which John was gathering experience.

This case went back and forth like a civil suit: request to the presbytery in April for a division, presbytery refuses; appeal to synod, reversal; presbytery appeals to General Assembly; town officials petition presbytery to withdraw appeal in the interest of peace in the town, presbytery refuses; town requests the two ministers to lodge a counter appeal against the presbytery, duly published in enormous detail; Assembly reverses synod decision. Result: the Laigh Kirk could not have its own separate session until its area of the town became a separate parish.

A more significant question arose: Could two elders who had been commissioned to General Assembly by Paisley be legally refused by the presbytery? Witherspoon appealed to the Assembly, which debated for two days. The outcome was to reverse the presbytery, seat the elders, and then decide that since "presbytery had excluded constituent members from voting, the entire election from Paisley was null and void and, therefore, the names of all Paisley representatives [were ordered] struck from the roll." We can only hope that Elizabeth had not accompanied her husband on that trip to Assembly. John had to sit through the whole session without a right to speak, no matter what outrageous statements the Moderates might be uttering. Small comfort at the moment that, as a result of this altercation, changes were made later to clarify commissioning of elders.

John's biggest legal battle of this decade dragged on for years. Known as the Snodgrass Case, it went the round of church courts and then moved into civil courts. It involved a large sum of money and, it is said, might even have prevented Witherspoon from coming to America.

In those days, on the Saturday evening before Communion there was a service to prepare members for the Sacrament on the following day. As the congregation was leaving the church on a Saturday early in 1762 someone overheard and reported to the minister that several irreverent youths were holding a mock Communion service near the church. Young Jack Snodgrass, a lawyer and sheriff's clerk, "used mockingly some of the words of the Institution of the Lord's Supper with a solemn air as of a minister."

Witherspoon took the matter up with the session, which sentenced the reprobates to "public rebuke before the congregation" plus whatever judgment presbytery saw fit to add. Presbytery, perpetually ready to disagree with John Witherspoon, did not consider sacrilege proven and released the young men with a rebuke. This struck Witherspoon as monstrous. He appealed to General Assembly.

He also had printed a sermon in which he had aired his view of the matter to the congregation. Though gently titled *Seasonable Advice to Young Persons,* the sermon had a subtitle that intimated what was to come: "On the Sin of Scoffing at Things Sacred." The work was offered for sale at bookstores throughout the country, and it nearly undid him. Friends who foresaw that it might persuaded him to recall the copies, which he consented to do while Assembly was meeting. But they were again released and sold from thirteen bookstores in various parts of the country.

So many read the pamphlet and reacted to it in Paisley

that the young men were not only ostracized but even threatened and physically attacked. Snodgrass put his legal knowledge to work. He sued Witherspoon for criminal libel and in June 1764 got a judgment for damages of £30. The court noted that the plaintiffs were guilty of improper conduct, thus justifying the sermon. But the publication naming names was "illegal, unwarrantable and injurious." However, the judgment was mitigated because the action had arisen from misplaced zeal rather than malice or injurious intent. On appeal Witherspoon suffered the ill fortune of having not only the original judgment upheld but the fine alarmingly increased—from £30 to £150, half again his annual salary, plus full costs.

Ashbel Green said that he had never heard of this affair! In writing the Witherspoon biography, Green asked several sources in Scotland for an account of it. One Thomas Crichton replied that he had been a child in Witherspoon's congregation in 1762. He remembered hearing the affair discussed more than once when sentiments strongly favored Witherspoon's positive action against an unthinkable act. Collins finally brought the whole sequence of events together. He went to His Majesty's Register House in Edinburgh and diligently combed over "archives . . . where the reader (if there ever be another) must struggle through reams of legal foolscap."

Jupiter Carlyle, interrogated by Crichton, averred that when Witherspoon came from America to Scotland in 1784 he was set upon by the son-in-law of one of the lenders and, unable to repay, was bailed out by a friend. Green actually saw a list in a notebook of Witherspoon's, a record of gifts from various friends amounting to about £40 toward settlement of the debt, but this has been lost. The case was not terminated until February 1776 in a compromise settlement.

Green devoted much space to this episode and strongly defended Witherspoon, saying that if he had ignored such mockery of a Sacrament, "he would have been considered by the whole of the pious part of his charge as criminally and shamefully shrinking from his duty; and would have irreparably injured his character, grieved his friends and incurred the reproach even of his enemies." Further, he quotes a guide to discipline for the Church of Scotland: "Scandals should be taken public notice of when they are of their own nature gross and infectious." And "worldly prudence . . . dictates the avoidance of personal trouble and inconvenience. . . . But Christian prudence is of a different character."

Green also notes that judges and lawyers tended to be Moderates, hence the courts may have been prejudiced. In John's own party the event may well have increased his reputation as an "unflinching repressor of vice, and advocate of evangelical truth and piety."

Defensible as the minister's action may have been in the eyes of the church where congregation and session strongly backed him, he was clearly wrong to have committed the civil offense of publication. The case naturally gave strength and comfort to his many enemies. As late as 1890 it still colored the judgment of another Scot, President James McCosh of Princeton. In speaking to a group of Presbyterians, he "implied that the Snodgrass case influenced Witherspoon in his decision to leave Scotland—his enemies were making it 'too hot' for him."

Collins believed, however, that McCosh was "merely paraphrasing earlier and mistaken writers." Not only was there a great show of regret at his departure, but it is incredible that the trustees in Princeton would not have known if there were real and widespread skepticism over John's honor. Had they known that, they could not have chosen him for their president.

The Paisley years saw for John not only a developing knowledge of ecclesiastical law and skill in argument but also a ripening theology. His large church was usually filled, and he was often invited to preach elsewhere. He wrote essays and articles that found a wide readership as well as did his published sermons. At least four of the sermons warrant attention as they flesh out and confirm his deepest convictions as a Christian.

The first was delivered in Edinburgh to the Society in Scotland for propagating Christian knowledge, in other words, a missionary society. The title of the sermon is uncompromising: *The Absolute Necessity of Salvation through Christ.* If any liberal minister is shocked by such an austere title, he might be the very one against whom the sermon is directed, a Moderate who woos his congregation with what to Witherspoon was sugarcoating. His plea was not to ease the message of the gospel in any way. It is of no use to disguise the fact that belief in Jesus Christ is the only path to salvation, and, he regrets, it is not superfluous to say so even to a congregation that calls itself Christian. His warning that toleration of any other point of view is not really Christian charity set off the Moderates. They raised dust in another literary skirmish declaring that John Witherspoon did not believe in charity.

To the sermon's second printing John attached an *Inquiry into the Scripture Meaning of Charity* to clear things up. The question is not alien today to us who tend to shrink from criticizing other church members' interpretations. Witherspoon points out that *forbearance* is one thing; *charity* is another. Referring to Paul, he affirms that we may withhold judgment of those who differ from us "in points not essential." But no Christian writer ever called this charity, which, John wrote, is "an ardent and unfeigned love to others and a desire of their welfare, temporal and eternal." Hence, should we find others in real error in their understanding of Christianity, it behooves us to take it up with them. Charity includes "the deepest concern for their dangerous state." To sit quietly, seeming to acquiesce, when a person sets forth a view at odds with the heart of Christian meaning would to Witherspoon be sin.

The next month, February 1758, his sermon, presumably in the Laigh Kirk at the time of the annual public fast, attracted attention with its question of our right to petition Providence for prosperity. The young preacher's conclusion is contained in his title: *Prayer for National Prosperity and for the Revival of Religion inseperably* [sic] *connected.*

"The evidence and the effect of an acceptable fast is repentance compleated by reformation," he asserted. Anyone can pray, and in catastrophes most people do; as we say, there are no atheists in foxholes. But Isaiah saw that God had no patience for this sort of thing when, at the beginning of the prophet's message, he inveighed against "vain oblations" and "solemn assemblies." To pray properly, Witherspoon observed, one must "have some measure of real religion." One must pray to honor God, not for immediate fulfillment of one's own wishes. One must have faith that "it may sometimes please God to make use of desolating judgment or alarming public strokes to awaken a secure thoughtless generation," and "dutiful, acceptable, and successful prayer for their removal can only be the work of his own children."

Further, John warned his congregation of the error that men make in relying on their own capacity to solve problems, "to put their trust in human prowess." If their own attempts come to nought, men are quick to blame "second causes," forgetting entirely "the supreme majesty of God." It is warranted, however, to use to their fullest extent one's own abilities, always recognizing that they will not be effective without "the divine blessing upon them." Such acknowledgment of our dependence will "prevent us from . . . idolizing and trusting" our own powers.

In September of the same year another sermon, sufficiently noteworthy to be printed in Glasgow and later in Belfast, Elizabethtown (now Elizabeth, New Jersey), and Boston, was delivered to Paisley Abbey at the ordination of a minister: *The Charge of Sedition and Faction against good Men, especially faithful Ministers, considered and accounted for.* Based on a text from Acts, "These that have turned the world upside down are come hither also," the gist of this message is that *good ministers must expect to have enemies.*

Pointing out that nothing is plainer in the Bible than the suffering of the good, Witherspoon asserts that "true religion being the same in substance in every age, we may expect to find a very strong likeness in all the real servants of God. . . . They have the same end in view, they tread the same path, and therefore must meet with resistance from the same enemies." David, Paul, Elijah, the Puritans, their own countrymen who obeyed God rather than man, all met hardship: harassment, prison, ostracism—at the very least, criticism; at the worst, death.

The very presence of a good man, Witherspoon suggests, is a judgment upon the wicked because "nothing can present peace to any man but some measure of self-satisfaction." A reproach, either actual or implied by better behavior than his own, will "disturb his dream and wound his peace." The reprobate reacts—in self-defense rather than malice, John generously observes.

Actual speaking and teaching of good things known to be true makes a man an even greater distress to those around him. Peter, John, Daniel, Shadrach and his friends, all ignored requests to stop speaking their good news and, of course, appeared "as disorderly and troublesome."

Most upsetting of all, Witherspoon warns his young colleague, is to "assert the truth and point out the errors opposite to it, with all their guilty fruit and all their dreadful consequences." To remain silent is to imply assent. Forthrightness will "either convince or provoke, reform or inflame," but one must risk it. And one must know that those "who love the gay and fashionable world incline to charge every profession of piety with hypocracy [*sic*]." Acknowledging that "many who are against ministers have been told that they are proud, factious, censorious, troublesome, mean," he reveals temperate patience in his next line: "Well, the thing is possible, no doubt."

He closes with an admonition: "If we are faithful to our duty, it will sufficiently provoke sinners, we need not add to it any mixture of human passion," for "the wrath of man worketh not the righteousness of God." And a consolation: "Triumph of sinners is but very short. In a little time all earthly relations shall be dissolved and the good shall come into their own."

*The Trial of Religious Truth by Its Moral Influence* was a topic that had already engaged him in Beith. He was strongly gripped by the text from Matthew, "By their fruits ye shall know them," and here he develops it even more powerfully than before. He acclaims this as "the best rule that could have been given." Most men, he points out, even simple and uneducated ones, know goodness when they see it, whether or not they know the philosophy underlying it. A long process of reasoning is no more likely—nay, may be *less* likely —to lead to truth than conscience. Anyone, "the meanest as well as the greatest," is endowed with this immediate ability to test a doctrine by its effects. Mere power to formulate a principle does not guarantee its results: "There often is great virtue and goodness in a mean capacity, and a great depravity in persons of eminent ability."

In actual fact, he points out, man uses this rule; he does judge by fruits. John would have liked the example of Abraham Lincoln's long walk to return six cents. Its strong appeal to generations of us bears out Witherspoon's contention that we do "try principles by their effects." Lincoln's act testified that honesty for him was not a mere word but a principle so much a part of him that it determined what he did.

Witherspoon read back from the actions of a good man to that man's acceptance of a fundamental truth that he embraced in the very heart of his being. In John's words, "There is something more in . . . every good man than barely a rational persuasion of the truth of religion," an experience that the gospel is true which is "more stable than any speculative reasoning." Conviction based on such an experience often can somehow communicate itself to others. When one is swayed by "the authority and example of others it is only their true probity, not mere eloquence which will survive in a man's character and influence others."

This is as close to describing the nature of John's own religious conviction that we find. Never has he hinted at any conversion experience. But this "something more . . . than barely a rational persuasion of the truth of religion, . . . more stable than any speculative reasoning" had a burning reality for him—to judge by the fruits.

All the works referred to thus far were printed singly. In 1764 a London publisher brought out in three volumes a collection of these plus *A Practical Treatise on Regeneration.* Entitled *Essays on Important Subjects,* the series provided a ready reference to a comprehensive statement of the Popular thought by its uncontested leader. Witherspoon had not in these works produced any new perspective to warrant attaching his name to a distinctive theology. His development of Scriptural texts combined his characteristic firmness with a lively awareness of the everyday world. It is likely that the large numbers of his listeners, won by his personal honesty and the quality of his life, were already inclined to read his words with assent. Those who were reading him with minds unresolved could find a clear statement of Christian doctrine, set down with order and sufficient variation to engage their attention.

This decade at Paisley was a time for growth of that mind and character already well rooted at Beith. Another satirical attack on corruption in the church is noteworthy for its atypical flight of imagination and for being the sole product of John's pen at that time which failed to attract much attention. Its title, even for the eighteenth century, was spun out to remarkable length with the usual enigmatic use of capitals: *The History of a Corporation of Servants Discovered a few Years ago in the Interior Parts of South America. Containing some very Surprising Events and Extraordinary Characters.* A supposed account of a social order in Brazil, its elements were fairly easy to identify with Scottish clerical structure, but it was

too elaborate and toppled of its own weight, for it had
nothing like the effect of *Ecclesiastical Characteristics.*

Witherspoon's name and fame spread sufficiently that he
was honored by degrees from the universities of Aberdeen
and St. Andrews. The town of Paisley awarded him in 1766
"a compliment of fifteen pounds Stirling" and six months
later raised his salary by twelve pounds. He also received
three calls to other churches. The congregation in Rotter-
dam received a quick refusal when it tried to lure him from
Paisley only a year after his installation. Likewise, he turned
down a call from Dundee, which should have settled the
matter. But never overlook the perversity of the Presbytery
of Paisley! If a certain one of its ministers said nay, it could
be counted upon to say yea. The town of Paisley, distressed
at the prospect of losing its minister, and perhaps knowing
which way the wind might blow in presbytery, petitioned
through its magistrates and council that the call from Dundee not be granted. This plea was seconded by a resolution
from the Society of Weavers, Taylors, Shoe Makers, and
Wrights in Paisley with an affirmation that the removal of
their pastor "would be much to the hurt of the Community
and Lay them under very great Hardship and Inconvenien-
cys." After due consideration, presbytery opined that reasons favoring the transportation to Dundee overrode the
objections; John should go.

When General Assembly met in May 1762, we see further
proof that Presbyterians did savor litigation. From Dundee
came two representatives of the magistrates and council
with three ministers of the presbytery and a lawyer to make
clear why Witherspoon should indeed move to Dundee
whether he wanted to or not. Up from Paisley came two
members of the town council with a lawyer as well as John
Witherspoon. The two cases were presented, the man in
question was examined, and the verdict rendered that he
should stay in Paisley.

One can see that Witherspoon had reason to insist on
what now seems obvious: that wishes of congregations and

ministers should be matched, and that it was senseless to ignore whatever natural affinity was present or absent. The usual difficulty was foisting a pastor through patronage onto a church that did not want him; this case was even more absurd.

Fortunately no questions were raised in the summer of 1766 when John told the church in Dublin that he preferred to decline their call. It was good to know that he was wanted, for by now there were plenty of Moderates to criticize him. Perhaps his critics and reverberations of the Snodgrass Case were the source of a rumor that was still getting into print more than a century later. It was that John was deeply disaffected with his native land and gladly left it. However, there is no evidence from him that this was so. Indeed, there is this considerable indication that he was remarkably appreciated by great numbers of his countrymen.

# 3

## The Wooing of a President

**1766-1768**

The Trustees . . .
chearfully . . . did elect
Dr. Witherspoon to the
President's Chair.

—*Minutes, the Board of Trustees of the
College of New Jersey, November 19, 1766*

Across the Atlantic, Presbyterians in America were also pulled into two factions but aligned on issues different from the Scottish. The colonies had been led into a Great Revival by George Whitefield during the 1730's. One group of Presbyterians, called the New Side, had been moved by a vivid experience of conversion. They began to find totally uncongenial the more conventional Presbyterians—the Old Side, centered in Philadelphia and its vicinity, whose faith leaned harder upon study and intellectual considerations. The Old Side looked askance at what began to be called "Enthusiasm" of the New Side (and of the New Light, a term for all "Enthusiasts," from whatever denomination). Once again in man's long history partisans of emotion and those of reason drew apart to survey one another with scowls.

Emphasis of the New Side upon personal religious experience and evangelism did not, however, preclude a strong wish to have well-educated ministers. It was only a conspicuous fringe who went to wild extremes of emotionalism, some of it quite outrageous, and seemed to rely little upon the discipline of training. Both factions wanted trained clergy. With no seminaries in the colonies, there was a distressing dearth of well-educated pastors, regardless of which side or light they manifested. The church had either to import young ministers from Scotland or to improvise. This was done by letting graduates of Harvard and Yale— the only colonial colleges besides William and Mary—add to their classical learning by reading divinity with some ordained preacher before going to pulpits of their own.

One center of this improvised teaching generated such animation among the New Side Presbyterians that, perhaps as much as any single factor, it led to the serious split from the conservatives. In Neshaminy, Pennsylvania, an Irish minister named William Tennent had four sons to educate. He must have been a winning man indeed, for all of them followed in their father's footsteps. Son Gilbert became leader of the New Side. Besides father William's compelling personality, his unusual mastery of Latin and lively exposition of divinity in instructing his own family soon attracted other young men. Before long, sufficient numbers were studying with him to warrant the building of a crude house on his farm for students and classes of what came to be known as the Log College.

The Old Side began to find these informal arrangements, repeated with variations at other parishes, intolerable. In these little centers libraries were meager, and equipment to study science nonexistent. T. J. Wertenbaker, writing of the Old Side critics, observes that "they asked scornfully, will it not bring religion into discredit to ordain half-educated enthusiasts, who lack the scholarly background to controvert the champions of other religious faiths or to recognize error when it lifts its head?" These were precisely *not* the primary aims of the New Side, who sought above all for their clergy to feel grasped by a power outside themselves. How could they *not* seek to persuade others once they had felt it? This was Enthusiasm, and it was fundamental. If one was possessed by it, evangelism was inevitable, and it could not be replaced by any college degree. Well, said the Old Side, maybe so. But probably not. In any case, these young fellows who have been getting their theological education from ministers scattered around the countryside will have to submit to examination. By us, of course. (Should this language sound too colloquial to record theological dissension, the reader might be assured that some of the language that emerged from this dispute was far more colloquial and considerably less gentle.)

In the end the protesting New Side Presbyterians were voted out of the Synod of Philadelphia in 1741. They turned then to sympathetic brethren in the Presbytery of New York, which invited them to unite with it. By 1745 all of them evolved into the new Synod of New York. Once the new synod was established, a small institution was started in the home of the Reverend Jonathan Dickinson in Elizabethtown, New Jersey, an indication of the rebels' earnestness for education. It was called the College of New Jersey, chartered after many difficulties in 1746 and opened for eight or ten students in May 1747. They used the library of their eminent president, who was well known as a theologian. His house was the college building, a few students sleeping in neighbors' homes. The Reverend Caleb Smith completed the faculty.

This brave beginning was tragically interrupted in less than half a year by the death of Dickinson. But so strong was the desire to see the institution flourish that the Reverend Aaron Burr (father of the duelist) stepped into the breach and invited the college to move to his home in Newark, only six miles distant. Burr, with devotion, energy, and intelligence, held this little cosmos together for three years without recompense. The enterprise got meager financial support from the New Jersey legislature, which was dominated by Quakers and other non-Presbyterians. Sporadic gifts and bequests kept it going. At last the number of students reached a point where new quarters had to be considered.

A site nearer the center of New Side territory was sought.

Word was sent out that the college would move into the town that, in return for advantages the institution would bring to it, would subscribe £1,000 toward a building and give land for a ten-acre campus plus two hundred timbered acres for fuel. Expectations turned toward New Brunswick, but, somewhat surprisingly, the conditions were met first by the tiny village of Princeton. To Princeton they would go!

The ensuing money-raising efforts toward a building started with a lottery for which Benjamin Franklin printed eight thousand tickets. This shocked the Old Side, who pressed—and won—a suit against gambling, which was illegal in Pennsylvania. At last Gilbert Tennent and another minister, Samuel Davies, were sent to obtain aid from churchmen in Great Britain. It was an eventful trip during which they kept running into opposition stirred up by letters from America written by members of the Old Side. They were pleased, however, to discover many who responded to their well-laid fund-raising plans. Davies even preached before the royal family and received a two-volume work on deism bearing the bookplate of H.R.H. George, Prince of Wales, who became George III.

Public relations strategy in that era used language quite different from the careful psychological designs that tend to emphasize the positive today. For example, the two men circulated a letter which included this desperate plea: "The young daughter of the Church of Scotland, helpless and exposed in this foreign land, cries to her tender and powerful parent for relief." It worked. As the men left the last town on their circuit they had more than they had dared hope for, some £2,200 sterling. Late in 1754 Tennent embarked for Philadelphia. Poor Davies, on a boat to his home in Virginia, suffered equally from severe storms and the crew's shocking profanity.

Two years were required to construct an appropriate building to house the College of New Jersey. Late in November 1756, while carpenters still hammered and plaster dried, President Aaron Burr and his handful of students moved into the largest building in North America. Nassau Hall housed in its basement a kitchen and dining hall and some rather dank cubicles which in a few years had to be used for students whose numbers were increasing at a gratifying rate. On the first floor were classrooms and a prayer hall where the college assembled to start the day, long before sunrise in winter. The library occupied the center of the second floor, with suites for study and sleep flanking it.

President Burr not only taught, conducted chapel, and kept track of finances and the endless details of even a small institution. As a prominent minister he also answered calls out of town for funeral sermons and speeches. As a result he literally worked himself to death only four days before the first commencement in Nassau Hall, September 28, 1757. Burr was widely and sincerely mourned. He had left a going concern whose quality and reputation drew students from many of the colonies.

Jonathan Edwards, Burr's famous father-in-law, was immediately considered for the presidency. He was summoned from his congregation and Indian mission in Stockbridge, Massachusetts. At the age of fifty-four, engrossed in his own work, Edwards reluctantly consented to move his large family 150 miles to the heart of New Jersey. The rejoicing that welcomed one of the greatest theologians America has ever had was all too soon silenced. Princeton was threatened with an epidemic of smallpox. Edwards was given an inoculation which was intended to induce a mild, immunizing case of the disease. But for him it was too much. Only a month after his arrival in Princeton he was dead.

Samuel Davies, who had proved his interest and ability to help the college in his trip to Britain, was then elected president. Through his refusal and reelection, it was fifteen months before he agreed to take up Aaron Burr's good work. Then "the tremor which seized . . . [him] at the thought of his situation" proved to be well founded. A year and a half of labor from dawn to midnight was more than his body, weakened by an earlier siege of tuberculosis, could sustain. He died in February 1761, having won especially warm affection and admiration for his character and achievements.

The Reverend Samuel Finley of Nottingham, Maryland, had graduated from the Log College. He tutored at his manse his own group of young men, one of whom was his nephew, Benjamin Rush. Finley was one of the first trustees elected to the College of New Jersey. He knew it well and was the logical choice to succeed Davies, which he did with distinction.

"With the death of Finley," according to Professor Wertenbaker, "the formative period of the college may be said to have ended. . . . Many graduates had gone out to fill important positions in civil life or to occupy the pulpits of New Light congregations from New England to North Carolina. Already the college had established the reputation which Princeton was to maintain for more than a century as the religious and educational capital of Presbyterian America."

With its 120 students upon whom depended many offices of leadership in the new land, the College of New Jersey sorely needed a man of strength, initiative, and, it must fervently have hoped, durability. It found the man with all three. But a long interval, with steps forward and jerks backward, passed before that man saw Princeton.

It is not known who proposed John Witherspoon to be the man to head the College of New Jersey. The trustees already had a meeting of minds on the subject when they met in 1766 to make their decision official. At that moment the Old Side produced a subplot to enhance our interest in this crucial development.

Old Side believers centered in an area farther south. First Church in Philadelphia was the focus of a group that had its own school to train ministers—in New London, Chester County, Pennsylvania. This was headed by a man of unquestioned ability, the Reverend Francis Alison. He had his troubles—one being a distressing tendency for his graduates to become Anglicans.

The College of New Jersey was in the ascendancy. The New Side at that time outnumbered its rival by more than 4 to 1. Morale and enrollment of the college were high, but there was one weakness that will hardly surprise any college administrator: funds were low. The construction of Nassau Hall had consumed all the capital, and, it turned out, income from fees was being handled with less than expertise.

This difficulty was known in Philadelphia, and when the trustees gathered at Nassau Hall in November 1766, a delegation from the City of Brotherly Love was there to present an amazing proposal. We see that communication then was not as difficult as we who can pick up a telephone might expect it to have been. The trustees already knew the mission of the Philadelphians: They were going to offer the olive branch to heal the breach, agree to underwrite salaries of four new professors, and supply a new president. For this *they* would choose the professors, and the president would be the Reverend Francis Alison. This was like the American Legion offering one of its members the presidency of the National Organization of Women.

The meeting was convened, and the first order of business was to receive the nomination of John Witherspoon as next president of the college. He was unanimously elected. Then the door was opened and the gentlemen from Philadelphia were invited in. The trustees listened with innocent faces as the visitors referred to the written proposals they were bearing. After their presentation they were then asked to leave while the trustees gave the matter "further mature consideration." Next day the news was out that the presidential vacancy had already been filled. The delegates from Philadelphia retreated in disarray, although the trustees did express hope for "harmony among all the friends and patrons of religion and sound literature."

This was not actually an empty expression, for the troubled waters of Presbyterianism were beginning to subside. Even Gilbert Tennent, before his death two years earlier, had become conciliatory. He might have found acceptable Witherspoon's deep spiritual conviction expressed in sermons consistently grounded directly in Scripture. John did not precisely identify with either Side, and his strengths could be admired by both. The Old Side, when it had time to cool off from the episode at Princeton, was sufficiently magnanimous to admit that it could consider Witherspoon a good compromise candidate. Not, however, without one parting shot: no one really knew much about Witherspoon as an educator.

The moment now seemed wonderfully propitious, not only to unite Presbyterians but to strengthen the one college of the middle colonies into a first-rate center of training for young men. The sort of decisions these young men would have to make no one could have foreseen. But the tale that might have been simply spun—of an invitation to Witherspoon, his acceptance, and arrival—became unconscionably convoluted.

A whole volume has been written on the subject, *John Witherspoon Comes to America.* Lyman H. Butterfield's absorbing account was inspired by an auction in 1943 of letters that Benjamin Rush had written as a medical student in Edinburgh, when he was unexpectedly drawn into the wooing of John Witherspoon to Princeton. These letters together with others form a documentary basis for the drama which, in brief, runs like this:

After the eventful trustees' meeting in Princeton in November 1766 a letter signed "William Peartree Smith Presdt. of Trustees" soon went forth to Paisley. It informs the minister of the Laigh Kirk that, "actuated by the most sensible Concern for the future Welfare of that rising Seminary (already become of unspeakable importance to Religion, and the Presbyterian Cause in North-America) under the late afflicting Providence, in removing by death their President, the Revd. & Worthy Dr. Samuel Finley, [the trustees] have employed their anxious thoughts, for several Months past, in looking out, both at Home & abroad, for a Gentleman, properly qualified, to succeed him in that important & conspicuous Station.

"Having maturely considered the various & important interests, which, under God, appear in a great degree, to depend upon the future prosperity of the College of New Jersey; and having considered also the Character You Sr. sustain in the Church of Scotland & in the Learned World —the Trustees, (this day convened for the purpose of election,) chearfully proceeded to elect and did elect Dr. Witherspoon to the President's Chair."

Acknowledging the sacrifice which he knows the change will entail, President Smith expresses hope that "the noble Cause you will promote in this Station of first Eminence in the Church in these southern Provinces, and great Ends your Compliance will answer to Religion & Learning in general thro'out all the Colonies, will afford You a more than proportionable degree of Satisfaction. And this Board do assure you that nothing in their power shall be wanting to render your Life here comfortable and Happy."

With a disarming frankness the letter runs through the fatal pathologies of the preceding presidents to show that their loss "hath been owing to *singular* circumstances" and that they thereby hope "to remove any apprehensions of the insalubrity of the Climate, which we can assure you is as healthy here, as in any part of N. America."

Besides the president's salary, the trustees could offer "a large hansome & commodious Dwelling-House . . . together with a good Garden & sufficient quantity of Land to furnish . . . Winter-Fuel & Pasturage." The total value was about £206 sterling, salary to begin the day he reached America, plus an allowance of one hundred guineas for moving costs.

Witherspoon was also told that at that moment one of Princeton's trustees was in London, and the board was asking him to go, if possible, to Paisley to give "the most authentic informations, and answer the minutest Enquiries." They assured Dr. Witherspoon that Richard Stockton was "a Gentleman of Fortune and Figure in his Profession of the Law" in whom "therefore Sir, You may place absolute Confidence."

Not only was Richard Stockton an outstanding citizen of the colony but his father, John, was one of the three men who signed the bond for £1,000 to bring the College of New Jersey to Princeton. He had sent Richard from Princeton to study with the Reverend Samuel Finley before his son became one of the first students of the college. In 1748 Richard graduated in Newark and remained to read law before he set up practice there. His ability attracted clients from other colonies, and soon he also had reading with him other young men, among them Elias Boudinot and William Paterson. The former became president of the Continental Congress, the latter a justice of the Supreme Court. Both would eventually be closely associated with John Witherspoon.

Stockton had exhausted himself in his work, which included riding to various courthouses for trials and maintaining the large estate he had inherited in Princeton. His doctor recommended a trip abroad. He set sail bearing a letter of introduction to a London publisher from Governor William Franklin, who could write as amusingly as his father, Benjamin: give him, he asked the publisher, "a sight of Samuel Johnson and a few more of your authors . . . for we Americans, when we go to England have as much curiosity to see a live Author, as Englishmen have to see a live Ostrich or a Cherokee Sachem."

Regard for Stockton's ability appears in his appointment to join Benjamin Franklin to work on Parliament to repeal its limitation on the issue of paper currency in America. Without it trade was difficult. When Stockton reached England he found Franklin established with his son in a spacious apartment, as busy with electrical apparatus and theory as with his mission for the colonies.

It was a slow business to convince Englishmen that America needed quick relief from its confused monetary system—or, rather, nonsystem. Forbidden to mint coins, each state had a paper currency of its own, with varying values against pounds sterling. Coins from whatever country a colony traded with were in circulation, and the Spanish pistole was almost as widely used as British shillings. It was a situation that the British Parliament could not imagine or cared about not at all.

Franklin had ample time to inquire into the facets of life that forever engaged him, and Stockton had opportunities for sight-seeing, collecting bulbs for his wife's garden, and various sociabilities. One young Englishwoman was moved to write that she took "an uncommon pleasure in his company" and found him "certainly the cleverest man I have yet seen from America." Into this pleasant scene arrived the letter from Princeton which bade him go to Paisley and make certain that the College of New Jersey would have a new Scottish president. A winter trip by carriage to Scotland held in those days no more attraction than a fall through the ice while skating. But Stockton went. Stopping first in Edinburgh to get the lay of the land, he proceeded west to Paisley. Late in February he and Witherspoon at last shook hands.

The two men liked each other. As Stockton outlined the assets and the needs of the College of New Jersey, Witherspoon's imagination was stirred. By the end of the visit his inclination was clearly toward assent. But into the smoothly moving machinery, sand was quietly poured. Elizabeth Witherspoon had not wanted to move from Beith to Paisley, a mere fourteen miles. How much less was she inclined to pack up household goods, five children, and say good-by, perhaps forever, to friends and family! She simply went to bed. She refused to expose her susceptibilities to whatever blandishments Stockton might offer. She declined to go to America.

The Princetonian, however, assured of the genuineness of John's interest, was not taking no for an answer when he left Paisley. He returned to Edinburgh to rally support,

which, curiously enough, he was able to do. The clergy
there who were friendly to Witherspoon were not eager to
lose their champion. But they too were interested in
strengthening Christianity filtered through the light of the
Presbyterian faith in the unknown continent to the west.
Not only had they met and talked with Tennent and Davies,
but their relationships with America were a good deal more
lively than we might conclude as we contemplate the sometimes months-long ocean voyage for every person, magazine, or letter that traveled between the two regions. Twelve
or thirteen years earlier at least one minister in America had
read at least one Witherspoon sermon. President Finley at
Princeton, only two years before his death, had thanked an
Edinburgher for "introducing me into a correspondence
with the Dear and Revd Mr. Witherspoon."

So on Stockton's return to Edinburgh from Paisley he did
not feel himself an utter foreigner. He had made friends
who welcomed and feted him and gave him the freedom of
the city. He took every advantage of his position to enlist aid
in helping him to change Mrs. Witherspoon's mind. To his
wife he wrote: "I have taken most effectual measures to
make her refusal very troublesome to her. I have engaged
all the eminent clergymen in Edinburgh and Glasgow to
attack her in her intrenchments, and they are determined to
take her by storm, if nothing else will do. . . . They were
upon my first coming . . . unwilling to part with her husband; but the light in which I have set affairs of the College,
has made them perfect proselytes."

A letter survives from one of those ministers who wrote
a long, stirring message to John, actually meant for Elizabeth. He generously showed her where *her* duty lay, quoting
freely from Scripture and indicating that if Sarah had not
accompanied Abraham, it would have been a sorry thing for
Judaism and Christianity. He did not hesitate to suggest
that "it is awful to cross the voice and will of God, . . . [and]
self will is extremely unamiable before man, and before a
Holy GOD most provoking."

Elizabeth was not moved.

Letters also arrived from America. One from an Old Side person in Philadelphia—"artful, plausible, yet wickedly contrived," according to Stockton—might have turned Witherspoon from considering the whole proposal. Others were warm and welcoming, with more and more information about that salubrious—how many times the word was used!—air of Princeton. (Apparently the town elevation gave it fewer mosquitoes than the surrounding countryside.)

Elizabeth continued her passive resistance. This kind of uprooting of her life called for more than gentle acquiescence. It needed a real taste for adventure, and that she did not have. She had borne ten children and was caring for five. She might have been just plain weary. By mid-April, Stockton, back in London and pressing John for an answer, elicited the word he least wanted to hear: no. John wrote his refusal painfully and reluctantly, indicating that at least his wife could now talk about the proposal. This had given him a degree of hope for change in her decision, but she "continued under Distress on the Subject," and he would push no further. He added that he would not elaborate on "the Persons who have given their Opinion and the Arguments used on both sides but it hath been a time of the utmost Anxiety and Difficulty to me."

This definite answer, far from closing the question, was just the sting to activate that impulsive, intelligent, attractive young Princeton alumnus, Benjamin Rush, then a medical student in Edinburgh. He had almost chosen the ministry himself, having read divinity with his uncle Samuel Finley. He was deeply interested in the church and knowledgeable about its affairs. He was convinced that John Witherspoon was meant for Princeton, and the refusal brought his immediate reaction: This cannot be! He laid aside his medical books to write to Paisley an impassioned letter which began "And must poor Nassau-Hall be ruined?" Witherspoon was desired in America for the very reasons that had inspired enemies for him in Scotland. Rush questioned whether Witherspoon could face his own conscience if he thus did "injury . . . to the College, to Learning, and to Religion in America." What position of equal interest and importance could Scotland offer? Furthermore, Americans would find it impossible to condone Elizabeth's refractory behavior which obviously interfered with her husband's duty. It was quite a letter from a twenty-two-year-old student to an eminent divine of forty-five. But it was mild compared to some of Witherspoon's incoming mail.

Mr. Butterfield observes that "the severity of the pressure to which Witherspoon was subjected at this time is suggested by his thanking Rush for the 'humanity & Politeness' of this letter as contrasted with the tone of other letters being received at Paisley. And the evenness of his temper amid these trying circumstances is positively inspiring."

Witherspoon, in his reply to Rush at the end of April, humbly declared that Paisley offered plenty to keep him busy, opining that "I am sure the Charge I have now is sufficient to employ another of greater Ability." He had no expectation of a better position in Scotland than what he had, for he "learned long ago that the Resentment of Enemies is always more violent as well as more lasting than the Attachment of friends and therefore never formed any Expectations that Way." He ends with an invitation to Rush to visit him.

The summer passed with John's mind still very much on America. He made two unsuccessful attempts to get other men to go in his stead (one had a wife who would not hear of it). He, with others, collected books for the library at Princeton. When Rush did visit Paisley in early summer, they became close friends. By August he was begging the young man "to make a jaunt this way." There was a persistent if unexpressed hope that between the two of them they might sway Elizabeth. He confessed to Rush, "I am held in the most painfull Anxiety and Suspence while there is not a Single Person here to whom I can communicate my Uneasiness." Two days later he wrote that he had, in effect, taken a deep breath and mentioned New Jersey to Elizabeth, who "was excessively struck with the bare Mention of it again as having believed it to be quite over & discovered the same or if possible a greater Aversion at it than ever plainly saying that such a Resolution would be as a Sentence of Death to her." He pressed Rush to come on anyway.

Rush went and soon was able to set down in his journal in an incredibly phlegmatic fashion these words: "After spending some days at his House we were so happy as to succeed in Our Persuasions." Eight months of suspense, worry, strategy, trips by stagecoach, decision, indecision, then—we "succeed in Our Persuasions," without even an exclamation mark! The only intimation of the nature of the persuasion lies in a single sentence of his memoirs written years later: "I lamented often in the presence of his wife his not accepting of the charge of the Jersey College, and obviated such of the objections as she had formerly made to crossing the ocean."

The only expression of the undoubted elation of Witherspoon and Rush is preserved by Archibald Wallace, their friend in Edinburgh. He wrote a letter on August 22 to Richard Stockton "to be forwarded with all Convenient Speed by Mr. Jonathan Smith Mercht in Philadelphia." This epistle sedately conveyed the news that Mrs. Witherspoon "has at last given a calm hearing to Mr Rush, argued the Matter with him, and received a satisfying Ansr to all her objections; so that now she is willing, if The Doctor is rechosen to the Presedents Chair in N Jersy Coledge, to go with him without Grudge, and will ask your pardon at Princeton, for the bad treatment she gave you at Paisley."

Between August and the next May when the family boarded ship at Greenock, John, with a new direction now clearly pointed in his life, was occupied with a myriad of concerns. He wrote frequently to Rush, now his close and trusted friend. Until confirmation from the trustees should

Witherspoon's letter to Benjamin Rush, August 12, 1767:

According to my promise I write You this Day but I have not yet been able to find a proper opportunity of speaking to my Wife on the subject proposed as she has been mostly ill since I wrote you last & could not go with me last week to Dundonald. On my Return yesternight I found her better & shall certainly mention it this Evening or to morrow so that if it be convenient for you to make a jaunt this way so as to be here Monday or Tuesday next we shall know the Utmost of it as it cannot be longer delayed. I am held in the most painfull Anxiety and Suspence while there is not a Single Person here to whom I can communicate my Uneasiness. I hope you will not fail to keep the Matter quite Secret.

be received, there was no one else with whom to share the secret of his acceptance. John also shared his amusement that the Moderates had interpreted Rush's visit to Paisley as a sign that he "was to bring it before the Church Courts and force me to go [to America] against my will."

Another trustee of the college also called at Paisley. The Reverend Charles Beatty had brought his wife to Scotland for medical treatment. His spelling in a letter to a fellow trustee, Richard Treat, who had a church near Philadelphia, raises doubt about the quality of the education of ministers then, but it contains the most detailed account we have of Elizabeth Witherspoon, a merciful revelation: "I was reluctant [to accept John's invitation to stay in his home] imagining I wul'd not be very agreable to Mrs. Wetherspoon, no more than she would be to Me, According to the Idea I had formed of her, however upon his Insisting upon it, I consented—& I must confess I was very agreably Disappointed, for Instead of finding a poor, peevish, reserved, Discontented &c—I found a well looking Genteel, open, friendly woman—which perhaps you'll be surprised at. . . . Before I came away [she] made some modest apology to me, for her conduct when Mr. Stockton was there, she appered to be concerned for it. She told me to this effect, that at that time & for some time before she was in a weak state of health, & in that Scituation things appered very gloomy to her—Crossing the Sea, & that her Husband, might soon die, & she be left in a strange country &c." Good Beatty for writing this! Good Treat for saving it! For this is almost the last word we have of Elizabeth and the only explicit word of her part in this whole long-drawn-out affair.

Charles Beatty preached twice on the Sunday he spent in Paisley, and Witherspoon "Lectured only." Beatty assessed him as "a good Speaker and preacher tho not a fine Speaker," and he "saw him make no use of Spectacles neither [in] publick nor private."

John passed through the same doubts of his ability to fill the presidency that Samuel Davies had experienced but he recovered his self-confidence. Butterfield remarks that "the tone of his letters [grew] steadily firmer. . . . The powers of leadership that all his friends knew he possessed [came] fully into play. He is now telling them what must be done, not they him."

He was especially concerned with gathering books for the library. He also met and talked with George Whitefield about the college that the evangelist was then establishing in Georgia. And he had a plan for "serving the Colledge by a certain means in Holland"—which never came to light. Butterfield surmises a possible union of the College of New Jersey with the Reformed Church's Queen's College (Rutgers) or at the least a Dutch professor of divinity for the faculty at Princeton.

Then came disturbing news from America. The trustees had not heard the news of Mrs. Witherspoon's changed disposition. At their meeting on October 1, in consultation with Old Side representatives, they elected another president! It was a curious action, not made decisively but as if they were still looking at Paisley from the corner of their eyes, listening for the sound of hooves heralding a rider who might pull John Witherspoon's acceptance from his dispatch bag.

The president-elect was Rush's classmate "Samey" Blair. He was twenty-six years of age, a minister, and nephew of a man they were appointing professor of divinity along with two other new teachers. Further, they determined that the new president should not take office for a year, nor would any of the three new professors join the faculty until funds were raised for their salaries.

Early in November, Witherspoon's acceptance reached Princeton. Richard Stockton responded to Witherspoon on November 5, putting forth his most tactful efforts as he explained what had occurred. The problem of easing Samuel Blair out of the office to which he had so recently been elected was delicate: "Mr. Blair has been informed that his youth will make him inadmissible among his Brethren upon

such Terms as he would chuse, and therefore before we
heard from Scotland it was generally said that Mr Blair was
so much disgusted that he certainly would not come in; but
now every one says that as he is as famous for his Modesty
as for his Learning and other valuable Qualifications he will
not hesitate to declare in the negative."

The paragraph ends with news of how joyful Princetoni-
ans are with the prospect of Witherspoon's arrival: "They
say it will effectually make up the ancient quarrell among
the Presbyterians here, will open a more easy & advantageous communication with North Britain &c &c &c. In short
your coming seems now the common Topic of conversation
and every one is pleased with the prospect."

This news was deeply distressing to Witherspoon, and he
wrote at once to Rush his "Concern this Circumstance gives
me." He regretted, in a mixed metaphor, that the trustees
had not let news of his own changed decision "go to
[Blair's] ears by private hands & waited for his spontaneous
Resolution. But how much more indelicate was it for any of
the Trustees to write to him & intreat him to resign." John
was considering whether, in this awkward situation, he
should resign—even though, *mirabile dictu!* "My Wife and
Daughter are now so much reconciled to it that I believe
they would be fully as willing to go as to stay."

Rush hurried to dispel the misgivings by assuring John
that not the trustees but Blair's friends in Philadelphia had
dissuaded him from accepting the presidency. They may
have said he had doubtless been voted in chiefly to keep
Francis Alison out of the position. John was still uneasy
about the treatment of Blair to which he referred more than
once in subsequent letters to Rush.

He did, however, continue developing plans for the college. He expressed hope for a science course that might
raise questions in youthful minds and set them upon the
road of inquiry rather than "to enter minutely into any
particular System." And the library was often mentioned.

There was then the reaction of Paisley to the step their

minister was about to take. Besides the expected regret, some parishioners proposed to go along to America, "so many," John wrote to Rush, "that I believe you must look out for an Island to settle a Colony." He began burning his bridges in February when he put his house up for sale.

In March he was off to London to consolidate ties with persons there who were friendly to America. And he hoped to see the king for sponsorship of an attempt to raise money before he left, but the king, wary of the bumptiousness of colonials, would not see him. John felt that "one that is to have the Direction of the Education of the youth of so considerable a body in the Northern Colonies deserveth some Notice."

In London he met an alumnus from Princeton from whom he "had the Mortification to learn . . . that at present there are but 50 students at the Colledge. In short every thing seems very discouraging." His spirits had occasion to rise, however, when "One Gentleman of his own Accord made a present of £100" toward the college library.

He did visit Holland before returning for the last farewells in Ayrshire. His old congregation at Beith invited him to preach one last sermon. His heart toward the Laigh Kirk was so full that his final sermon to them on *Ministerial Fidelity* required two Sundays to deliver (with two services each Sunday? A memorable sermon!). Benjamin Rush, almost a doctor now, came to the meeting of presbytery at which John requested his demission from Paisley and, representing the college, the young alumnus bore the minutes of the trustees' meeting in which Witherspoon had been unanimously elected president.

At last on May 18, Captain Robert Spier of the brigantine *Peggy* welcomed onto his ship Elizabeth and John, followed by Ann, now 17; James, 16; John, 10; Frances, 8; and David, 7. Before the anchor was raised, Dr. Witherspoon had time to write a last word to Rush, regretting that he could not use the last sayings of Samuel Finley in his final sermon. Benjamin had sent them by a courier who unfortunately stopped too often to refresh himself on the way and arrived too late. There were final greetings to a few friends, the last mentioned of whom is Miss Annie Hogg.

For more than eleven weeks the *Peggy*, with no stabilizers and no Dramamine aboard, made her way westward. Ann and John, Jr., had birthdays during the journey but how or if they were celebrated we do not know. It was August 6 when a pilot boat tied up at the wharf in Philadelphia with news that into the Delaware was sailing the little ship bearing the Witherspoons. This was stirring news, for by now the name was known up and down the coast. Citizens hurried to the river to hail the ship from boat and horseback. The Witherspoons' new and unknown countrymen waved and shouted greetings to the family from the shore.

# 4

## President Witherspoon

> Use your authority for God
> and he will support it.
>
> —*Letters on Education,*
> *John Witherspoon*

### 1768-1776

Mrs. Witherspoon's first fortnight in America must have allayed many of the misgivings that had so long postponed their arrival. She had no doubt of her husband's position in Scotland, but how could she have guessed that so many Americans knew who he was?

In the year and a half since John's first election, there was ample time for most of the Atlantic seaboard to have heard of developments at the College of New Jersey. Presbyterians were acutely interested in a resolution of their denominational disputes. More trained ministers were acutely needed to serve the Scottish immigrants then spreading into the Alleghenies and Appalachians. Indeed, religion and education were of importance to people throughout the colonies. Once news on either subject reached an area, word of mouth could be counted on to spread it. Timely delivery of letters and newspapers was improved significantly when, more than a decade earlier, Benjamin Franklin became Deputy Postmaster General. He had greatly strengthened a postal system that had regular routes from Maine to South Carolina.

Trustees of the college, scattered between New York and Philadelphia, did their share in spreading the name of Witherspoon. One of these, the Reverend John Rodgers of the Wall Street and Brick Churches in New York, with an excitement no doubt passed on to his parishioners, wrote an impulsive letter to John just after his first election. Revealing his own and others' hopes, Rodgers assured John that "the President of the College of New Jersey . . . will sit revered at the Head of the Presbyterian Interest allready great and dayly growing in these Middle Colonies. And no Man can have it more in his Power to advance the Cause of Xtian Liberty by forming the Minds of Youth to proper Sentiments on this most interesting Subject."

Letters from the ebullient Benjamin Rush were surely quoted in many a conversation in Philadelphia. A publisher there had recently offered a new edition of *Ecclesiastical Characteristics*, an opportunity to savor directly the quality of John's mind and values. This publication struck many readers as a familiar picture of certain American clergymen. Even a Unitarian minister in Boston thought it would be all to the good if "every minister in America would read it at least once a month."

Hence, it is not surprising that when the *Peggy*'s hawsers were made fast and the gangplank was in place, Philadelphians competed for the honor of lodging the family. A merchant, Andrew Hodge, won the privilege of entertaining them for five days while they regained their land legs before the last short lap of their journey. In this interval many knocked at the door of the Hodge home to greet and to see for themselves the first "imported" college president, whose very education and experience in Europe brought its own prestige.

At last, on August 12, the family bade good-by to their new friends and climbed into the stagecoach for Princeton. As they rolled through farmland and woods, curiosity no doubt was mounting concerning the place that was about to become home for the rest of the lives of the parents, as well as for Ann, whose husband would succeed her father as next president of the college. When the coach reached the broad Delaware it passed onto the ferry and at the other side rumbled off into Trenton. There a party of trustees living in the vicinity, together with interested friends, welcomed the family to New Jersey. Some ten miles farther, the driver had to pull up for a sizable crowd lining the road. Here was the whole College of New Jersey! Students, faculty, and Vice-President William Tennent—joined by a number of townspeople—had come to the Province Line Road to convoy the travelers the last two miles into the village.

With few trees in town and none on the campus, perhaps the newcomers caught a glimpse of the college before they turned short of it into Morven. There the door swung wide and the Stocktons received them to stay until the president's house on campus was readied for them. That night the warmhearted reception was complete when they strolled from Morven down the short block on Nassau Street. Nassau Hall glowed with a candle placed in each window by the students in one last gesture for this very full day. John's surprise and appreciation at the character of his reception by the town and college were expressed the next Sunday in his first sermon in Princeton.

Adjacent to the president's home a Presbyterian church had been built four years earlier for a town-and-gown congregation. Townspeople occupied the pews, and the gallery was for students and visitors. The college used the building for its commencements, and the president assumed preaching and pastoral duties besides those usually assigned to a session. Witherspoon appears to have had a warm relationship with the group, although he missed the stimulus of his large and diverse Scottish flock.

Would that some attic in Paisley or Beith might yield a letter or two written from Princeton during the month that followed! John's first recorded personal reactions came from a trip upon which he embarked in early October. The businessmen on the board of trustees were apparently not assiduous overseers and had left details to administrators who, it turned out, were not experienced administrators. The result was that the steward was deeply in debt, half of the small endowment was not invested, and students were in arrears with their fees. Two months after Witherspoon's arrival the trustees had to borrow money to pay his salary. Money was the immediate need. John at once tidied the books by requiring advance payment from students. This made possible a reduction in the annual fee to £23.13, New Jersey proclamation money, for everything—tuition, room and board, firewood, and candles. But bigger money was needed.

Raising funds is not a talent that anyone noted in John during his life in Scotland. Yet he set out promptly, with vigor and confidence, to extend his acquaintance and spread the message of the needs and potential of his college. In September he preached in New York—and impressed one minister as "but an indifferent Figure in the Pulpit." The critic was Anglican, but even Presbyterians had never compared Witherspoon as a preacher with his ancestor Knox. Early in October he started a month's journey through New England, where he preached four times in three days in Boston. He returned with £1,000 from Bostonians, including gifts of £100 each from the three Phillips brothers whose names are still perpetuated at Exeter and Andover. There were hints that further gifts might follow.

The presbytery and synod also asked for congregational subscriptions to aid the college. During Witherspoon's first three years, the little church in Princeton gave a handsome total of £1,400. General collections for the college were made in South Carolina and throughout the Synod of New York and Philadelphia. Gifts from Georgia were made in produce, and the college had to charter a ship to bring it north. A trip to Williamsburg in 1769 brought out crowds too large for any church. John's sermon delivered in the capitol yard brought a collection of £86. Gifts came also from other parts of Virginia, that bastion of Anglicanism.

The College of New Jersey, 1764

Before long the college was in the black, although still lacking sufficient endowment to support the new professorships Witherspoon hoped for. In fact, he himself became the professor of divinity which he knew the college must have if it was to train ministers adequately. In April 1769 the board voted John an increase of £50 in salary to compensate for his added responsibility.

As president and teacher, Dr. Witherspoon was faced with another sort of problem—philosophic idealism. Bishop George Berkeley's three-year stay in America several decades earlier had left its effects on the philosophy taught in some American colleges. Berkeley's attempt to reconcile science with religion had led him to conclude that the world and its contents existed only in the mind. "To be is to be perceived" summarized his observation. All we can be sure of is what we know through our senses. What is beyond them, what may actually exist as objects in the physical world, we cannot prove.

Witherspoon soon found that Berkeley's philosophy was appealing to various educators in America. Samuel Johnson, president of King's College (Columbia University), had taken it up with enthusiasm. John Periam, a tutor at Princeton, found its novelty engaging, and Samuel Stanhope Smith, another Princeton faculty member, was likewise attracted. These young professors, with a few of their interested students, were reading such books with the title page removed to conceal their heretic venture.

Witherspoon soon scotched the pursuit of this will-o'-the-wisp. In characteristic vigor he wrote, "I affirm . . . that the ideas we receive by our senses and the persuasions we derive immediately from them are exactly according to truth, to real truth, which certainly ought to be the same with philosophic truth." He was firmly against deductive reasoning from assumed principles. Truth, as he saw it, began with data received through our senses and was attained inductively with an accumulation of experience. John once mentioned to Green that in an article in the *Scots*

*Magazine* he had some years before attacked idealism on the same grounds later set forth by Thomas Reid and James Beattie in what became known as the Common Sense philosophy.

At least one historian of American thought found this position less than admirable. Woodbridge Riley's conclusion on the Witherspoon influence on Princeton reads: "The spirit of common sense left little to the imagination, desired no novel inventions, but preferred to keep its adherents revolving in the treadmill of traditional thought. In fine, the policy of the New Jersey College was to turn out safe minds content to mark time in the old way." Samuel Johnson, looking down upon Princeton from his urban locale in New York City, called the College of New Jersey "a fountain of nonsense."

To unbelievers, Christianity itself is a fountain of nonsense. The bases of it are not for reason to deal with. Witherspoon had been selected to preside over a college which, though not a seminary, would train Presbyterian ministers. Neither a speculative man nor one given to playing with ideas, he saw his commission as turning students directly to the truth as Presbyterians of the time saw it. Thus it was said that "Scottish realism held the Atlantic States as a private preserve and Princeton College was its hunting lodge."

A significant bonus from the fund-raising trips lay in President Witherspoon's encounter with Americans and their country. He was delighted with what he saw. He liked Yankees and he liked southerners. He started a long-lasting friendship with President Ezra Stiles of Yale. His encounters in the south drew many students to Princeton. Washington in 1769 sent one of his young relatives to Princeton. The impression Witherspoon made on James Madison's father led to his son's enrollment also.

In 1770 Witherspoon wrote to Colonel Henry Lee in an easy conversational manner that shows his concern for individual students: "I have nothing to add to what I wrote formerly of the behavior of your sons, and their progress in their learning. It has always been in all respects agreeable. If Joseph Cross does not pass . . . shall add it to this letter."

In his American travels, a Scotsman was bound to observe that "the sky in America appeared much farther away than at home and was not continually falling in moisture." The neatness of the villages, the productivity of farms, the evidence of self-respect and independence in men of all occupations deeply impressed him. John thought all of this was decidedly superior to Scotland's poverty-stricken areas where sharp class divisions made lesser men even more miserable than did their mere lack of wealth. Before long he was making active moves to encourage the immigration of Scotsmen to a country where they could better their lot. He preached to raise money to support immigration and twice entered into plans to acquire land for settlements of Scots in the New World.

With Richard Stockton and others, Witherspoon invested in land in Nova Scotia to colonize Scots. The most decisive part he seems to have taken was to retain veto power on land prices, ostensibly to prevent speculation. Of livelier concern to him was a similar development in Ryegate, New Hampshire, later a part of Caledonia County, Vermont. He occasionally visited this settlement of Scots, preaching and baptizing. His son James built a house for himself there when he graduated at Princeton.

More than once John was accused of being a land speculator. The otherwise friendly President Ezra Stiles of Yale calculated in his diary that Witherspoon's annual rental income was "£5,000 ster. annum." The calculations upon which Stiles reached that glorious sum did not, however, rest on fact. A century later Princeton's President Maclean also saw John as a sharp dealer in real estate.

In 1792 Witherspoon was still holding twelve thousand acres in Nova Scotia. Aware that he was suspected of being a moneygrubber, he wrote to the *Scots Magazine* that he had made no money nor was he hurting Scotland by encouraging emigration. "What is it for a man to be a friend to his country?" he asked. "Is it to wish well to the stones and the earth, or the people who inhabit it?" Scotland's difficulty was not that anyone was luring people from it, he bluntly told his readers; Scotland's difficulty was land monopoly with its outrageously high rents and its repression of farmers to perpetual tenancy, hopeless of ownership. The letter, indeed the whole episode, is one of the first evidences of John's interest in an area wholly outside theology, education, or church government.

By March 1772 a major appeal for college funds was planned for an area that today might be low on the list of the development office: the West Indies. In those islands were many Englishmen whose incomes from sugar and molasses would enable them to afford an American education for their sons. Charles Beatty, the visitor to Paisley earlier, was chosen to go on a tour of supplication to Jamaica and other islands with James Witherspoon, only twenty years old and two years out of college. The expedition came to a quick and tragic end. Charles Beatty contracted smallpox shortly after they reached "the Barbadoes" and died there. James returned to Princeton with no additions to the endowment. However, it did happen that in the following years a number of students from the West Indies made their way to Princeton and studied at the college. They may have been attracted by a document that President Witherspoon had printed for the two men to take with them.

An *Address to the inhabitants of Jamaica, and other West Indian Islands in behalf of the college of New Jersey* describes fully the curriculum and aims of the college as well as some of its peculiar advantages, including, of course, the salubrious air. In Ashbel Green's judgment, "the character and claims of the college are stated . . . with great delicacy and ingenuity" in this tract. It is, in fact, a well-drawn sketch of the institution and a considerable revelation of its president. Using the *Address* as a guide, we may flesh out from other sources a fair portrait of the college a few years after John's arrival.

An outline of courses contained in the *Address* gives a quick insight into the program of the college, remarkably similar to curricula in Britain at that time:

| Freshmen: | Juniors: |
|---|---|
| Latin and Greek | Latin and Greek |
| Roman and Greek | (to some extent) |
| antiquities | mathematics, |
| Rhetoric | natural philosophy |

| Sophomores: | Seniors: |
|---|---|
| Latin and Greek | higher classics |
| Geography | mathematics |
| (with use of globes) | natural philosophy |
| philosophy | moral philosophy |
| mathematics | |

Graduate degrees were also offered. Three years' post-graduate study could lead to the "Masters and such other degrees as the trustees think fit." This possibility could better "fit young Gentlemen for serving their country in public Stations," for the ministry, or for the practice of law or medicine. Such diverse possibilities meant that, contrary to some misconceptions, the College of New Jersey was not a seminary. Having stated this, we must acknowledge that prayers which started the college day in freezing darkness at 5:30 A.M. were compulsory. There was no option to be a practicing atheist by lying abed.

Witherspoon himself lectured on chronology and history, composition and criticism, and taught French to those who wanted it. Before graduating, every student would have heard twice over the lectures in the former two subjects. This lecturing was an innovation, a new method at which some looked askance. Could a student learn simply by hearing a talk? Didn't he need to apply himself to a text which he could read and reread? Until Witherspoon came, the students had done that. Classes consisted of questioning by their teachers, who might then add whatever enlightening comment or exposition they wished. But assigned reading was still the focus of education.

Witherspoon's innovation drifted back to the old method as he became absorbed in other duties. Each student then made a copy of each lecture, using these as a text. These lectures Green remembered studying until "every leading idea contained was fixed in the memory." The recitations were enhanced and "frequently enlivened by anecdotes and remarks" by Witherspoon. He made it so interesting that after fifty years Green still remembered some of the president's observations. The student was also impressed that his professor "never forgot his character as a teacher of religion—one of whose principal inducements in coming to this country was to educate men for the gospel ministry."

Public speaking received close attention. Every evening after prayers two or three students would take their turn on a stage in the prayer hall and "pronounce an oration . . . that they may learn by early habit presence of mind and proper pronunciation and gesture in public speaking." Each senior wrote and delivered an oration every five or six weeks for "all persons of any note in the neighborhood." Then ambitious orators had their great opportunity at commencement, which took place on the last Wednesday in September.

At commencement in 1769 John Hancock of Boston received an honorary master's degree. He heard student speakers vying in conspicuous eloquence which drew upon their heads a disgruntled opinion from one hearer that "in no country are there so many orators, nor so many smatterers." Witherspoon appreciated the value of practice in public speaking, but even he commented on the "warm, passionate declamations," indicating that he would prefer more light and less heat. In his *Lectures on Eloquence* he urged students to consider "a plainer manner of simple oratory."

A number of seniors always spoke at the graduation exercises, but the day before was given over to contests for any student who wished to compete in "pronouncing English orations" and other events. The whole day was a sort of intellectual Olympics, with three prizes for each contest decided by the vote of all college graduates present. The competitions included: "reading the English language with propriety and grace and being able to answer all questions on its Orthography and grammar," reading Latin and Greek, speaking Latin, and something described as "Latin versions." President Witherspoon conducted the Latin contests himself, one of which might be based upon "a Newspaper from the pocket of the President" or from a marked passage in a book for the competitors to put into Latin, without dictionaries, in a given time. Ashbel Green recalled that "this Latin competition, which was always ardently contested, appeared to afford great gratification to the literary company by which it was witnessed."

The commencement oratory addressed a wide range of topics: "Civil Liberty is necessary to give birth to the arts and sciences," "Moral evil does not take away the perfection of the world" (in Latin, so not everyone could have been convinced), "Advantages of Health." Professor Wertenbaker credits Witherspoon with an admirably progressive attitude in encouraging students to consider political questions, although he received heated criticism for the youthful impulsiveness in some of the political speeches.

A writer of a letter to the editor of the *Pennsylvania Chronicle* in 1772 was dismayed at "the [Princeton] graduating class discussing 'the most perplexing political topics,' which they solved 'with a jerk.' " In his opinion, colleges were for contemplation of ancient states with a scrutiny of their cultures and constitutions, not—heaven forfend!—of "the British constitution or the present circumstances of the nation." Students, he thought, should spend a quiet interlude in college, learning to "distinguish truth from falsehood and . . . to compose with accuracy and elegancy and to speak properly and persuasively." But this gentleman was in the minority. Throngs crammed every inn and home in Princeton, appearing to enjoy the commencement contests and orations as well as taking pride in their own special graduate. Witherspoon described those visitors as "a vast concourse of the politest company from this province, New York and Philadelphia."

Commencement began with an academic procession formed at the president's house. Headed by the graduating seniors, it was brought up in the rear by the governor of New Jersey. The stately parade was set in motion by the president's command, *"Progredimini juvenes!"* which began the short walk to the Presbyterian church next door. Once settled in their seats, the company heard the president pray. Then he recited the ritual words: "Doctors and gentlemen, these young men wish to greet you with an oration."

Whatever sedate observations of such an occasion might be made by faculty or visiting parents, a student in the audience might see a rather different picture. The year 1773 has gifted us with a letter from a student, William R. Smith, to a graduate of the preceding year, Philip Vickers Fithian:

> Fe-O-whiraw, whiraw, hi, fal, lal, fal, lal de lal dal a fine song —commencement is over whiraw I say again whiraw, whiraw.
>
> And what is more never was there such a commencement at princeton before and most likely never will be again. The galeries were cracking every now and then all day—every mouse hole in the church was cram'd full—The stage covered with Gentlemen and ladies amongst whom was the Governor and his lady; and that he might not appear singular Lee was stiff with lace, gold-lace—[A student then, he was later known as "Light Horse Harry" Lee.]
>
> A band . . . from Philadelphia assisted to make all agreeable and to crown the whole eloquence of Demosthenes was heard in almost every man's mouth, so that the person who spoke last was always the hero of the tale—O murder! what shall I do I

want to say a great deal to you but cannot for the girls who are almost distracting my heart— . . .

—then more about the distraction, less about the commencement.

When William R. Smith collected himself after his celebration (at the Hudibras Tavern?), he too might have admitted pride on an object upon which President Witherspoon enlarged in his letter to the Jamaicans. The scientific equipment of the college was, he claimed, "equal, if not superior, to any on the continent." A special coup was the president's procurement of William Rittenhouse's first orrery. This complicated mechanism sent brass and ivory models of planets around the sun at their correct relative speeds, demonstrated the moon's eclipses as it rotated around the earth, and displayed Saturn with its rings as well as the progress of Jupiter's satellites. The orrery attracted a wide interest and was talked about wherever educated men came together. When it was finished in 1771, it had been assumed that Philadelphians would buy it from their talented townsman for the University of Pennsylvania. But the alert Witherspoon consummated his purchase for £416 and had the orrery in Princeton before the Pennsylvanians knew what had happened.

A grammar school connected with the college "under the particular direction and patronage of the President" might also have arrested the attention of the Jamaicans. The grammar school had existed and died before Witherspoon came. He was aware of its significance for the college, and in Britain he had discussed what was needed for such a school. "Within one week after his inauguration," Collins records, he had completed his plans, obtained the sanction of the trustees, chosen a member of the senior class—William Churchill Houston—as master, and published an advertisement in the papers stating that the school would open in November with the beginning of the winter term of the college.

This adjunct was a common necessity, and, into the twentieth century, it could be found at some colleges. Because students came from varying backgrounds and there was no College Entrance Examination Board, most colleges had prefreshman courses to help assimilate students into college work. The grammar school at Princeton, unlike some, accepted even students not intending to finish college. Extra courses were offered for them, including French taught by the president. A significant clue to his attitude toward teaching lies in his note that a terrestrial globe aided the preparatory pupils "by occasional exercises for amusement rather than for a task." Other passages show that he worked for active responses from his pupils rather than attempting always to be didactic.

The West Indians were treated to more than an exposition of the college program. Witherspoon is often exhortatory as he perceives advantages of college in general. Children of the rich, he notes, especially need "an early, prudent, and well conducted education" to preserve them from the "dangerous temptation" of wealth. Education will also help them with duties that their affluence puts upon them and will preserve them from "vices of a certain class, . . . inspiring the mind with an abhorrence of low riot, and contempt for brutal conversation." More positively, college training is a necessity for "those who do not wish to live for themselves alone, but would apply their talents to the service of the public and the good of mankind."

He pleads that New Jersey is closer to the Indies than Britain, of a better climate, and can, in its smaller institutions, offer more personal supervision of students. With all students living in hall, no one can pretend sickness and stay away when examinations are given.

Discipline at the college, the president notes, is "by reason and the principles of honour and shame." There is no "correction by stripes" but censure is given in a planned progression of degrees: from the president, a professor, or a tutor in private; the faculty; the young man's whole class;

the whole college. If the last named fails to reform him, he is expelled.

The College of New Jersey is nondenominational, and he declares concerning some who have left the college, "I am wholly uncertain, at this hour, to what denomination they belong." The independence of the college from church or powerful donors frees it from having to "chuse teachers upon ministerial recommendation or in compliance with the overbearing weight of family interest." Likewise, those in charge are freed from "any temptation to a fawning, cringing spirit and mean servility in the hope of courting favour or promotion." As for political involvement, he warily says that a college "ought to be not deeply into political contention. . . . But surely a nation which naturally tends to produce a spirit of liberty and independence . . . is preferable to the dead and vapid state of one whose very existence depends upon the nod of those in power." His immediate request to the Indies is for funds to establish professorships, and he ends with an appealing fillip: "The short lives of the former presidents have been by many attributed to their excessive labours, which it is hoped will be an argument with the humane and generous to lend their help in promoting so noble a design."

As the *Address to the Jamaicans* was never properly delivered by his emissaries to the Indies, Witherspoon paid a Philadelphia newspaper to publish it in full. This novel venture into advertising drew growls in print from both New York and Philadelphia. The writer in New York saw in the reference to family influence on a college a veiled sneer at King's College. He resented the whole appeal for new students, remarking sarcastically that "the Youth of North America were to be lured by the Charmer's Voice into the Bosom of Nassau Hall" away from other colleges. The injustice of the charges baited Witherspoon into an answer to the *New York Gazette.*

He held his peace toward the Philadelphia writer whose arguments were similar, plus a smug observation that the college in Philadelphia had been the first to seek students from the West Indies; Princeton was belatedly imitating its ingenuity. Another Philadelphian issued a whole pamphlet against the brazen claims of Witherspoon. He took a firm stand against independence of thought which, he noted, always led to turbulence. He also thought it unbecoming for the president to boast about his graduates. And he for one questioned the beneficence of Princeton's climate.

An interesting if unresolved footnote to this period appears in an address to the Rhode Island Home Missionary Society in 1903. The Reverend T. Calvin McClelland, with enough specifics to sound credible, reported that in 1774 "two bright, steady Christian colored men by name Bristol Yamma and John Quamine . . . were matriculated at Princeton college under the tuition of President Witherspoon." They were to be sent by Rhode Islanders to Guinea as missionaries. Princeton has no record of these men, but they could have been special students of the president.

When Witherspoon was invited to Princeton, Francis Alison's questioning of his ability as a teacher was not impertinent. The only visible sign of Witherspoon's interest in education per se was a letter on *The Education of Our Children*. Dated 1763, it was followed in 1775 by four more. By 1822 the letters had been reprinted eight times in America and in Britain. Containing specific advice on teaching even babies, the letters reveal a close scrutiny of children, their parents, and many determiners of how a person grows. Concerned with formation of character more than scholastic mastery, the letters may have affected early-nineteenth-century families.

Some of Witherspoon's observations would be readily endorsed today. Both parents, he felt, should reconcile their own thoughts on child-rearing, for "want of concurrence . . . is easily observed even by very young children." Consistency is a bulwark against juvenile tyranny. He does not comprehend parents who "ask pardon, at least give very general marks of repentance and sorrow" for reprimands or punishment. This, he remarks, only irritates the child and provokes more untoward behavior. The foundation of good discipline is a parent whose own behavior is a worthy model and who is "not fretful or impatient or passionately fond of his own peculiarities." To seal the effectiveness of discipline, Witherspoon admonishes, show affection and kindness whenever the child's behavior permits.

Less popular now would be his minute directions for training a baby to accede without rebellion to his father's wish. He details a successful experiment in quietly removing from a baby's hand some cherished object until the father wins total compliance of the little one.

The overarching influence set forth by Witherspoon, again not prominent in twentieth-century educational theory, is to be expected from a Christian minister: "Use your authority for God and he will support it." Instead of admonition, show a child a pertinent passage from Scripture, and the sought-for end will "generally be accomplished with prayer for his blessing. I know well," Witherspoon characteristically admits, "with what ridicule this would be treated by many if publicly mentioned but that does not shake my judgment in the least."

Some do not connect piety and politeness, he notes, but "true religion is not only consistent with but necessary to the perfection of true politeness," which is by no means confined to the *haut monde* but may be found in "the remotest cottage of the wildest country." In pious country people, there is "a certain humanity and good will attending their simplicity." Religion is not only "the great polisher of the common people," but "it even enlarges their understanding. . . . Having been accustomed to exercise their judgment and reflection on religious subjects, they are capable of talking more sensibly on agriculture, politics or any common topic."

Christian conviction should, for the benefit of the young, enter into all social relationships. "What we see every day has a constant and powerful influence on our temper and carriage." No parent today who is attempting to hold off from his child the vulgarity and rudeness in our culture would contradict this. Witherspoon finds that entertaining strangers in one's home is a great teaching device, for children quickly notice whether we "esteem others not according to their station or outward splendor but by their virtue and real worth." As for conversation, expressing thoughts "with modesty and candour . . . will keep you at an equal distance from a surly and morose carriage on the one hand, and a fawning, cringing, obsequiousness or unnecessary compliment and ceremony on the other." Finally, he warns against receiving "guests warmly and the moment they are gone falling upon their character and conduct with unmerciful severity." He has seen children pick up this spiteful habit and have it nourished by families who do not recognize that "there is no disposition to which young are more prone than derision . . . and few that parents are more apt to cherish, under the idea of its being a sign of sprightliness and vivacity."

The letters end with further emphasis that "general truths, however justly stated or fully proved," have small effect unless the person offering them lives as if the truth made a real difference to him. "If you want children to learn, behave as if you consider religion as necessary, responsible, amiable, profitable, delightful." Further, children will conclude, if one is "sparing of the mention of heaven or hell, . . . that a neglect of their duty is only falling short of a degree of honour and advantage, which, for the gratification of their passions, they are very willing to relinquish. Many parents are more ready to tell children such or such a thing is mean, and not like a gentleman, than to warn them that they will thereby incur the displeasure of their Maker." If one is Christian, one faces the conclusion that "unless we are reconciled to God we shall without doubt perish everlastingly."

He finishes with pastorly suggestions to parents on how they may nurture their own faith to produce the example so necessary for their children's training. Going through motions of religion will not do, and yet where does one start? "It is a very nice thing . . . to know the connection between spirit and form. The form without the spirit is good for nothing; but . . . spirit without the form, never yet existed."

He suggests some forms: Observe the Sabbath in church and with family; visits with friends will merely be distracting. Visit the sick and dying; talk to them, show your concern for them, but—as on all occasions—be slow to speak and swift to hear. Treat servants well but not familiarly. If you are a politician, you have special opportunities; be "firm and incorruptible . . . for promoting . . . the good of mankind." He rejoices—with all of us—in "that man who has principles, whose principles are known, and whom everybody despairs of being able to seduce or bring over to the opposite interest. As for your placeboes," he goes on, "your prudent, courtly, compliant gentlemen, whose vote in assembly will tell you where they dined the day before, I hold them very cheap indeed."

These letters offer clues into the character of Witherspoon the father, the disciplinarian of students, the pastoral counselor, the politician. They depict, finally, a man who did not shrink from making a harsh judgment even if he made enemies by it. The last letter includes a statement that "religion is generally the most powerful as well as the most uniform principle of decent conduct." This was undoubtedly his true belief and standard. His performance in his various roles may be measured against it. This standard may also help us to sort out from his vigorously stated convictions a few that we tend to dismiss with a smile as outmoded manners of a period. Could it be that they are truths which in our time have been distorted or forgotten?

The most pointed test of how well Witherspoon's actions fitted his words on education is lacking: some expression from an outsider about the Witherspoon children. Ashbel Green, however, details examples of Witherspoon's discipline of students, both in principle and in particular. Green and one of his classmates became tutors at the college as soon as they had graduated, and as they started their new duties, the president gave them, as Green recalled it, this advice:

> Govern always but beware of governing too much. Convince your pupils, for you may convince them, that you would rather gratify than thwart them; that you wish to see them happy, and desire to impose no restraints but such as their real advantage and the order of the college render indispensable. Put a wide difference between youthful follies and foibles, and those acts which manifest a malignant spirit, and an intentional insubordination. Do not even notice the former except it be by private advice. Overlook those entirely unless they occur in such a public manner that it is known that you must have observed them. Be exceedingly careful not to commit your own authority or that of the college in any case that cannot be carried through with equity. But having pursued this system, then in every instance in which there is manifest intention to offend, or to resist authority, make no compromise with it whatever; put it down absolutely and entirely; maintain the authority of the laws in their full extent, and fear no consequence.

Green offered examples of President Witherspoon's ability to apply these principles. He ignored harmless pranks, administered wrath but not punishment when deluged by a bucket of water intended for a student, and with "an appearance that was truly awful" confronted the whole student body in a real crisis that ended with his judgment upon the leader: "You, Sir, are expelled; and go you immediately out of the Hall." In fairness and freedom from personal animosity Witherspoon thus "gained the affection and confidence of his pupils."

The college trustees could justifiably beam upon one another at their choice of their sixth president. With no experience connected with a college, he had fitted in the role of administrator and educator as perfectly as an egg in its shell. He had won respect and affection for himself as a man and as a teacher; he had put the college on its feet financially, had shown interest and initiative in equipping it with books and apparatus, and had kept continually before everyone his principles as a Christian not only in his sermons but in his life.

Concurrently with his work as a college president and professor he had a wide range of other involvements. He preached; he wrote—more often on secular than on religious subjects; he became a developer of sorts to encourage emigration from Scotland; and his quality as a political man shifted from the ecclesiastical contentiousness in Scotland to wrestling with other Americans on questions of government and war.

# 5

## New Jersey Sidles Toward Independence

The revolution was in the minds and
hearts of the people, and this was
effected from 1760 to 1775 . . . before
a drop of blood was shed.

—*Diary of John Adams*

**1770–1775**

Americans, John Witherspoon found, were not a whit less
disputatious than Scots. They argued in taverns and living
rooms and newsprint. They fought about boundary lines,
religion, education. They went to court with actions of all
sorts. In fact, Collins slyly observes, during the period in
which the colonies were moving nearer the break from England, when the day came that New Jersey lawyers recommended minimum litigation in order to free men for public
service, "the loudest Tory scoffer must have perceived that
New Jersey was becoming thoroughly earnest."

It is a true marvel that colonists with so many internal
quarrels drew together to win a war and to create a nation.
But powerful cohesive forces among early Americans did
exist. Two, noted by historian Edmund S. Morgan, were
their ownership of property and their tillage of soil. In no
other country on earth did so large a proportion of persons
have title to homes and land. The psychological result was
a shared protectiveness for their possessions. The almost
universal engagement in agriculture also provided strong
bonds of common interest. Even city dwellers had kitchen

gardens and often owned farms as well as urban residences.

President Witherspoon was no exception. He purchased a farm visible at that time from the campus, a mile to the north of Nassau Hall. One summer afternoon in 1772 a visitor found him working his fields with some of his students on what he hoped to be a scientific study of agriculture.

The next year he replaced the farmhouse, which had burned, with a stone residence which is still standing and lived in. He called it Tusculum after the town on Lake Albano near Rome where Cicero and others owned country villas. He offered it for rent in a notice in the *Philadelphia Journal* of August 1773. The advertisement describes the two-story dwelling with four rooms on each floor, which "will be very proper for any family who choose to reside for sometime in that agreeable country, for health or pleasure, or who desire to have the education of their children carried on under their own eye . . . but the Proprietor being fond of agriculture and engaged in a scheme of improvement, will not let any of the lands for tillage." There is no sign that the proprietor became any Luther Burbank, but his acreage and stock supplied the family table and himself with exercise and a happy alternative to academic routine.

The farm also furnishes a miniature verbal portrait of its owner, left in the report of a lady who was shown the premises by John. At her exclamation that there was not a flower on the place he firmly replied: "No, Madam. No flowers in my garden, nor in my discourses either."

This area had earlier charmed the Swedish traveler Peter Kalm, who wrote that between Trenton and Princeton he "never saw any place in America, the towns excepted, so well peopled." The abundance was overwhelming and "we were always welcome to go into the fine orchards and gather our hats and pockets full." He liked the Dutch barns, huge structures with low walls and high roofs. He commented—with disappointment?—that one could spend half a year in Philadelphia without seeing an Indian. Near Princeton "one

Witherspoon's farmhouse, Tusculum, still standing and occupied

might have imagined himself to be in Europe."

An especially fine farm, widely known for its excellent gardens, honey, and wheat, belonged to Colonel George Morgan. His house was some three hundred paces back of Nassau Hall, on the site of the future residence of Princeton presidents. The size of the village is vividly intimated in Colonel Morgan's home address: Prospect-near-Princeton.

Richard Stockton would have been lord of the manor had this been England. His grandfather had bought, mostly from William Penn, five thousand acres in the neighborhood. The Old Dutch Trail, now Stockton Street, passed before Morven, his home which dominated the town with its hunt breakfasts, little teas, and great dinners. Its extraordinary garden with exotic trees and a grotto was patterned after Alexander Pope's, which Richard saw on the same trip that took him to the Witherspoons' in Paisley.

In 1755 Richard contracted with Elias Boudinot's sister Annis a marriage that was unusually happy. The nineteen-year-old bride was put to an unaccustomed test: her husband's seven orphaned brothers and sisters, ages six to nineteen, shared their home. Annis cherished the children and capably managed the slaves who helped her. In due time her own four daughters and two sons were added to the household. She was an intelligent, vivid, energetic, warmhearted woman. She wrote poetry which, though lacking the pointedness of Emily Dickinson's, pleased her contemporaries and was often in print. Morven's hospitality rivaled that of Mount Vernon, whose heroic proprietor was, in fact, one of the long train of Morven's guests: the seven Witherspoons, ambassadors, noblemen, generals, and on one historic day the whole Continental Congress.

Annis' reference to "wagon loads of peaches" summons a vision of the bounty of Morven's well-cultivated land—in fact, of products of the whole vicinity. Into this peaceful scene two armies were to march, one after the other, overrunning the village.

On July 13, 1770, a public hangman was hired by the students at the college to burn a letter. James Madison, a student himself, wrote that they stood about in academic gowns while the tolling bell of Nassau Hall drew attention of townspeople to the outrage of this particular item. The letter, intercepted by means not specified, notified Philadelphia merchants that New York merchants chose not to heed the nonimportation agreement.

The students rightly guessed that their president would not interfere. Several years before his arrival, the graduating class had attended its commencement in clothing of American fabrics by way of saying "We don't *have* to buy British." Repetition of this political demonstration at succeeding commencements won the endorsement of Witherspoon. An unknown observer saw in it a potential influence upon "the lower ranks of mankind." He found a sterling example in the "young gentlemen of fortune and education, many of whom will probably shine in the various spheres of public life, who would thus voluntarily throw aside those articles of superfluity and luxury which have almost beggared us."

The occasion for the native-spun clothes was the Stamp Act, passed in February of 1765. During the decade that followed, the colonists had as many variables to weigh, with consequent changes of mind, as a man deciding to leave an alcoholic wife. One prominent consideration was the recurring declaration of loyalty to the Crown. Convening bodies of protest and written expressions of indignation pleaded not for a severing of ties but for a changed attitude of Parliament and the king toward the colonists. It was ten years before independence appeared to be unquestionably the only course—and that decision had more than enough dissenters.

An interesting segment of New Jersey history lies in Collins' chapter on Witherspoon's part in "Undermining Colonial Government in New Jersey." In the two and a half

Signer of the Declaration of Independence, Richard Stockton

. . .and his wife, Annis

years between December 1773 and July 1776, tentative actions full of questioning and uncertainties gradually became decisive steps.

On December 16, 1773, when the Boston Tea Party sent waves of emotion up and down the seaboard, residents of Nassau Hall lugged out of the steward's storeroom his winter's supply of tea. They burned it and whooped around a bonfire, which consumed also an effigy of Massachusetts' Governor Hutchinson, a tea canister around his Tory neck. The president remained unshaken by this outburst, but the trustees found it "unwarrantable and riotous." They denied commencement honors to its chief instigator, who would have been valedictorian.

Like fallen limbs at a river's edge, the colonies one by one were lifted on the rising waters of antipathy to Britain and drifted together as they moved downstream. Massachusetts and Virginia floated sooner than New Jersey. But uneasy colonists had begun to look toward one another and ask how it was with their neighbors. In the summer following the incineration of the letter, New Jersey, like Virginia and New York, formed committees of correspondence to exchange information between towns, counties, and states on local events and developments in Parliament pertinent to America.

When Somerset County, which then contained Princeton, formed its committee of correspondence in July 1774, there was no doubt that the president of the college would be a member who could be counted on. A major activity of his adult life had been to frame opinion on controversial questions and to choose his side without temporizing.

One of the committee's duties was to join their corresponding numbers from eleven other counties to select delegates for a proposed congress which would bring together grievances and decide upon action. For this purpose, 72 men of the province met in New Brunswick and drew up resolutions that bore a strong mark of the Witherspoon pen. Beginning with the accustomed affirmation of loyalty, the resolution protested taxation without representation and parliamentary acts against Massachusetts; they recommended a general colonial congress, an agreement of nonimportation and nonconsumption, a collection of money for those who had suffered in Boston; and they elected five delegates to the Continental Congress.

John was not one of them but was as absorbed and as responsible as if he were. He proceeded to clarify his own ideas in an essay entitled *Thought on American Liberty,* written soon after the meeting at New Brunswick. Acknowledging that the Continental Congress would be a break with familiar political organization, he claimed for it a basis upon the law of reason—from which issue all laws and customs that hold people together in any nation. The coming congress, he thought, should draw the colonies together to defend themselves, if it came to that, from being forced to submit to injustice. He suggested positive actions to the colonies by way of manufacturing, of attracting emigrants, of strengthening militia, and—an interesting appeal—to warn British military men of risks they personally would run if they tried to enslave America.

This was Witherspoon's first written work on the American controversy. He had respected the specific request of his synod that clergy not use pulpits as platforms for political exhortation, but his conversation and his tolerance of students' patriotic expressions left little doubt of his position.

This position rested upon a respect for personal liberty, popular government, and honest expression, whose roots were implanted in him in Scotland. This was the man who had vehemently protested the Moderates' suppression of a congregation's freedom of choice and their imposition of a minister chosen by the patron. This was the man who had warned a young minister that good men follow their own consciences—and are charged for that with "sedition and faction."

Witherspoon was remarkably free from prejudice against

England. His conflict in Scotland had been directed against other Scots, not against Anglicans. His journey to London before he went to America suggests a friendly reception there. Indeed, his first collection of essays was published in England, not in Scotland. *Ecclesiastical Characteristics* had been appreciated by English bishops. And in 1777—of all times!—his sermon on the *Dominion of Providence,* which the Scots had roasted, was benignly reviewed in the British literary magazine *Monthly Review.*

In Massachusetts, involved persons were farther downstream toward the cataracts of war. John Adams was churned by strong feelings and doubts. In late June 1774 he admitted to his diary: "I muse, I mope, I ruminate. I am often In Reveries and Brown Studies.—The Objects before me, are too grand, and multifarious for my Comprehension. —We have not Men, fit for the Times. We are deficient in Generals, in Education, in Travel, in Fortune—in every Thing. I feel unutterable Anxiety.—God grant us Wisdom, and Fortitude!"

On August 10, Adams and three other delegates left Boston at eleven o'clock in the morning for Philadelphia. Their destination had not even a proper name. It was variously called the General Congress, the Grand Congress, the Congress of Deputies, or the Congress at Philadelphia. When we think of the Continental Congress, we assume great honor attached to it, forgetting that some elected delegates refused to go—and that Georgia sent no one.

But from Boston to New York, concerns were keenly focused on this gathering. Again and again the coach in which Adams and his friends rolled was surrounded by citizens who convoyed them into town, talking all the way, questioning and informing. At their first stop, "kind wishes and fervent prayers [were offered] . . . for health and success. This scene was truly affecting, beyond all description affecting," wrote Adams.

At New Haven a throng on horseback and in carriages met them, and bells tolled as they entered town. In New

York they were feted for several days, and leaders of the area called upon them and entertained them. The delegates eagerly enlarged their understanding of local problems and learned something of the prominent men of each vicinity. New Yorkers asked interested questions—then impetuously continued the conversation without waiting for answers. Adams found them rude.

From New York their route took them over four ferries before they reached New Brunswick for a brief look around. Then, about noon on August 27, they jolted into Princeton and put up at "the Sign of the Hudibrass, near Nassau Hall Colledge." (The Hudibras Tavern was the object of an impromptu excavation by local archaeologists in 1969 when an underground wing was being added to Firestone Library and workmen began running into cups and glasses.) By the time they had finished eating, a student, son of a Massachusetts friend, presented himself and "took a Walk with us and shewed us the Seat of Mr. Stockton." Adams found the library "not large but has some good Books." They inspected the orrery, "a most beautifull Machine" and "electrical Apparatus which is the most compleat and elegant that I have seen"—gratifying testimony from a Harvard man.

After prayers in the chapel, they met the president. He "took them to the Balcony [cupola] where there is a view 80 miles in diameter. Then to the President's House for a Glass of Wine." A salient topic of their conversation was Witherspoon's earnest conviction that Britain utterly mistook American attitudes toward their situation. The English stubbornly failed to grasp that Americans yearned for justice, not separation. Parliament appeared downright deliberate in its refusal to hear reason in American protest. To remedy this, Witherspoon forcefully proposed a practice much later to be labeled "public relations." Earnestly, he insisted that America should hire English writers to explain America to Britain in their own newspapers.

When they set down their empty glasses, "the Doctor

waited on us to our Lodgings and took a Dish of Coffee." In the evening another student reported that "the Government of this College is very Strict, and the Schollars study very hard. The President says they are all Sons of Liberty."

Next morning John Adams went to church. The diary entry reads, "Heard Dr. Witherspoon all Day. A clear, sensible, Preacher." Unfortunately, though, "the Schollars sing as badly as the Presbyterians at New York." Jonathan Dickinson Sergeant, an alumnus and treasurer of the college, joined the visitors for supper and further extended their background by sharing what he knew of all the lawyers from New York to Virginia. He commented as well on men they were about to encounter in Philadelphia. "He says the Virginians speak in Raptures about Richard Henry Lee and Patrick Henry—one the Cicero and the other the Demosthenes of the Age."

Next day they moved on. At Frankford "a number of Carriages and Gentlemen came out of Phyladelphia to meet us." There were Mr. McKean of Delaware, Mr. Rutledge of Carolina, and a number of others. One was Benjamin Rush, who got into the carriage and as they rolled over the last stretch began a friendship with Adams that was to outlast the war. When they reached town, "dirty, dusty and fatigued as we were we could not resist the Importunity, to go to the Tavern [City Tavern, modeled after one in London], the most genteel one in America."

Into this stimulating gathering of men of varying backgrounds and interests, acquainting themselves with one another in preparation for the task they had come for, John Witherspoon arrived five days later. Instead of moping that he was not a delegate or blowing off steam in a letter to the editor of the *Pennsylvania Gazette,* John followed the advice he later gave Ashbel Green in another context: "Go you down to Philadelphia." Totally wanting in apprehension that he might be considered an outsider, he went to the City of Brotherly Love. Dr. Edward Shippen, a trustee of the college (who had been summoned to give the ill-fated inoculation to Jonathan Edwards), welcomed President Witherspoon to his home for a breakfast gathering which included his brother-in-law Richard Henry Lee, whom Adams called "a masterly Man."

Witherspoon seems to have fit the company quite comfortably. In referring to the breakfast party, Adams remarks that "Doctor Witherspoon enters with great Spirit into the American Cause." The fraternizing continued, Adams tells us, when later he "spent the Evening at Mr. Mifflin's with Lee and Harrison from Virginia, the two Rutledges, Doctor Witherspoon, Dr. Shippen. . . . An elegant Supper, and We drank Sentiments till 11 O Clock. Lee and Harrison were very high." Witherspoon was as close to the unfolding events as it was possible for him to be at this time.

The first Continental Congress formulated Articles of Association through which committees of observation permitted a kind of vigilante action toward citizens who were not subscribing to the articles. Criticism of Congress, drinking tea, or otherwise breaching the articles might lead to blacklisting, boycott, or at the very least a grave talk with members of the committee. Committees also directed melting of lead for bullets and forming and drilling militia.

In December 1774, Witherspoon was again placed on the new committee of correspondence of Somerset County. This was to meet with committees of other counties and, lest omissions occur during transition between old and new political structures, to appoint delegates to the next Continental Congress if the assembly did not do so. (Called the General Assembly, it met by proclamation of the governor and achieved whatever self-government Britain allowed the colonials. The name is identical with but unrelated to the annual gathering of the Presbyterian Church.) However, the assembly met the next month and dismayed Governor Franklin by approving actions of the Continental Congress and reappointing its state's delegates.

In the spring came the stand of the minutemen. It was five days after that exchange of shots that a rider galloped into Princeton at six o'clock in the morning. Before he rode on to Trenton and Philadelphia, a trustee of the college and its steward had endorsed his dispatch and sent out excited ripples of news which reached the farthest edges of the community by breakfast.

It was essential for the province to know whether its people stood together and agreed upon next steps. To discover this, a Princeton town meeting convened that day and asked for a provincial congress to replace the assembly. President Witherspoon surely attended and participated in the meeting, but he was not one of the 19 delegates elected to the congress that met at Trenton on May 23, 1775. However, nine were from Princeton, some associated with the college and fully able to represent the president's sentiments.

Even in the tension of that hour, the provincial congress did not act hotheadedly. It realized the danger of a breakdown in civil order that could occur between two different governing bodies. The assembly of 87 had just adjourned, and only 7 of these appeared also at the provincial congress. The congress solemnly considered its obligation to proceed with deliberation and—unlike many another revolutionary body—listened to one member's plea to "support established civil authority for the maintenance of order and the undisturbed administration of justice, as far as was consistent with the preservation of fundamental liberties." Aware of the implications for themselves and future generations of their decisions on "life, property, religion and liberty," the delegates agreed to open each session with prayer. Eager not to be at odds with the Continental Congress, they dispatched William Peartree Smith and Elias Boudinot to Philadelphia to consult with that body upon moves it wished to recommend but for which no guide had been written. The provincial body then approved resolutions of the congress regarding cessation of fish exports and followed congressional direction for writing articles of association.

Small wonder that Governor Franklin wrote to England

with alarm! He feared that there was not even a British ship nearby to evacuate loyalists should a dire need for escape arise.

Dr. Witherspoon's first decisive role in the Revolution was as a clergyman. He headed a committee of the Synod of New York and Philadelphia to write a letter in that eventful month of May 1775. One of the most striking pronouncements of the period, the letter expresses the concerns of the minister, the political man, and the educator that John was. Addressed to Presbyterian ministers of the synod to release them from the apolitical silence previously imposed, the letter reveals Witherspoon at his earnest best: with war now inevitable, there is no question of pacifism; Christians will fight, and their belief will free them from fear of death; they will be humane and merciful on the field of battle and show the meekness and gentleness of spirit which characterize real valor; they will observe fasts and pray regularly; when not engaged in military action they will lead moral lives, pay their debts, and help each other. And— Christians are noted for paradoxes—they will show allegiance to the king, support the Continental Congress, and maintain the union of the colonies. John Witherspoon revealed the widespread ambivalence of his time. He still thought of himself as a Briton. He wanted to be loyal; but he could not accept the condescension, the face turned from the supplicant American, the closed door to reasonable request, the total injustice consistently dealt to the colonists. The letter was distributed through New Jersey by the hundreds, but no copy remains.

On the secular side, he continued moving nearer the center of activity. In July 1775 he became chairman of the Somerset committee of correspondence. When the provincial congress adjourned in August, its committee on safety —actually an executive committee to act in the interim between sessions—held its meeting in Princeton, where it doubtless received Witherspoon's opinion.

On the clerical side, his baccalaureate sermon in Septem-

ber 1775 on *Christian Magnanimity* became a cachet for
President Witherspoon. He repeated it on baccalaureate
Sundays, with variations, for some ten years. With only
oblique reference to political agitations, his message was a
solid statement of practical results of being a Christian.
Being a Christian, he pointed out, enhanced other endeavors such as education, making war, making friends. His
theme was that simultaneous development of Christian virtues and social skills in an individual are reciprocal in their
effects. A college education is—or should be—catalytic for
learning which can continue throughout life. Association
with others in friendship, for social or religious ends, en-
hances the endeavors of them all. He had observed in Edinburgh that outstanding persons flourish in clusters, stimulating one another. Likewise, Christians need one another,
and faith flourishes in community.

Following the October session of the New Jersey provincial congress in 1775, a shift occurred from the old colonial
government to a complete assumption of responsibility by
new institutions. The committee of safety, which governed
the state until the next congressional meeting in January,
ignored the old assembly, and took over its barracks to
house its own newly recruited troops.

Governor Franklin, still trying to hold on, called a meeting of the assembly in November and asked whether the
Crown officers should abdicate and flee. Its answer revealed
that the brave events of rebellion among Jerseymen did not
rise from a unanimous sentiment. It promised the governor
loyalty for another year and assured him that the seeming
commotions around the state were of little consequence;
there was no reason for him to be fearful. The governor was
informed enough to be more annoyed than encouraged by
the reply, and the next week he suspended the assembly
forever.

The assembly had voted to direct the Continental Congress to do its best to wrest a satisfactory response to
colonial complaints, the basis of which the assembly did not

deny. It also urged every effort to avoid a break which would lead to a new government. The question that separated the two factions in New Jersey—as in all the colonies—was not whether they had been wronged but whether they should try once more to redress grievances. The provincial congress made a decisive vote in February 1776 when eleven of twelve counties voted for independence.

The Somerset County committee of correspondence, driven by its chairman, John Witherspoon, made a variety of moves and suggestions. Seeking a ton of gunpowder from Philadelphia for the arms it had collected might have been expected. Promoting fairs for the sale of linen was more novel. Witherspoon wanted to see the colonies develop their own industry and free themselves from dependence upon imports. Manufacturing textiles seemed to Witherspoon a practical way to enable many to be productive and through their earnings to enrich the whole state, ultimately the nation. Unfortunately, the project did not succeed.

Witherspoon's solid contribution in this prerevolutionary era lay in his writing, his speaking, and his understanding that great events of all kinds begin in the minds of men. One measure of his influence may be read in the bitterness of a satire against him written by an agitated Tory, an Anglican minister of Burlington, on *The American Times*. Five stringent stanzas are aimed at Witherspoon, who, we may confidently guess, enjoyed them immensely. Excerpts reveal the depth of the Reverend Dr. Odell's desperation:

> Ye priests of Bael . . .
> Mess-mates of Jezebel's luxurious mess,
> Come in the splendour of pontific dress;
> Haste to receive your chief in solemn state;
> Haste to attend on Witherspoon the great.
> ...............................................................
> Princeton received him, bright amidst his flaws,
> And saw him labour in the good old cause;

Saw him promote the meritorious work,
The hate of kings, and glory of the kirk.

. . . unhappy Jersey mourns her thrall;
Ordain'd by vilest of the vile to fall;
To fall by Witherspoon—O name the
curse
Of sound religion and disgrace of verse.
..............................................................

Fierce as the fiercest, foremost of the first,
He'd rail at kings, with venom well-nigh
burst;
Not uniformly grand—for some bye end
To dirtiest tricks and treason he'd de-
scend.
I've known him seek the dungeon dark as
night
Imprison'd Tories to convert or fight;
Whilst to myself I've hummed in dismal
tune
I'd rather be a dog than Witherspoon.
Be patient reader—for the issue trust,
His day will come—remember Heav'n is
just.

Odell also refers to four attempts of John's to "overset
the laws." One was an extraordinary event which Elias
Boudinot set down in his diary. When the trustees met at
Princeton for two days in April 1776, the president was
mysteriously absent on the second day. At the conclusion of
the early morning meeting, Boudinot and William Peartree
Smith mounted their horses to return to Elizabethtown. In
New Brunswick they stopped to rest their horses and heard
that county representatives to the provincial congress, in
response to a newspaper notice, had assembled. Who
should be addressing them that afternoon but Dr. Witherspoon! This transplanted Scotsman had decided to lobby
strongly for a complete break with England, and he spoke
for an hour and a half, exposing the delegates to the convic-

tions that gripped him. With characteristic self-confidence, he had summoned the representatives to come to *him.* Also characteristically, he expounded his position not with fire but in what the opposing Boudinot, with commendable objectivity, judged "a very able and elegant" speech.

However, the conservative Boudinot took strong exception not only to Witherspoon's conclusions but to the situation in which he and Smith found themselves. It seemed to say that the trustees of Princeton were underwriting this performance, two of them conspicuously present at a meeting of which they would seem to have known and approved. At the conclusion of John's address, Boudinot rose and gave a strong counterproposal that efforts be left in the hands of the Continental Congress, which had been duly elected, to determine the course of New Jersey after facts had been assessed and opinions gathered throughout the state.

Witherspoon, undaunted and following the rules of debate, started a rebuttal. Someone whispered to him that he was seriously disturbing his friends the trustees, and he immediately desisted, swiftly concluding in an admonition to representatives to consult their own constituents. By this episode he earned a judgment that he "was far in advance of his province even in April 1776 in his effort to 'overset the law.' "

The next month he made one of his best-known public statements, this time from the pulpit. On Friday, May 17, 1776, businesses were closed and people thronged to churches to observe the public fast designated by Congress, disdainfully called "Congress Sunday" by Tories. Congress asked people to pause and look soberly at the total change about to come into their lives. Hostilities had started a year ago, but only now did a consensus for independence seem imminent. On that day, from Maine to Georgia, ministers were confronting their congregations with the implications of a declaration for independence.

The whole college and most of Princeton swarmed into

the Presbyterian church on campus. Dr. Witherspoon rose
in his black gown with white Geneva tabs and for a good
hour preached on *The Dominion of Providence over the Passions
of Men.* He did not take undue advantage of the freedom
now allowed by his denomination. With restraint for such
a known partisan, he was two thirds through before he
mentioned his political position, and he did not linger over
it.

What Dr. Witherspoon said was what he had always said,
the Christian message in a Calvinist frame, resting firmly on
Scripture. It included sufficient comment on specific human
traits and the immediate dilemma to reveal clearly a
preacher who did not live alone among his books. He was
acquainted with human foible, for which he had a certain
compassion but never condoned.

The text, not precisely transparent, was from the Seven-
ty-sixth Psalm: "Surely the wrath of man shall praise thee:
the remainder of wrath shalt thou restrain." This signified,
Dr. Witherspoon indicated, that rage and unreason, with all
their tragic consequences which make man's life miserable
for himself and for those on whom he works out his feelings,
are yet the potential source of his salvation. When he brings
life to its lowest ebb—by his own unthinking behavior—his
desperation impels him at last to change. Confronted by his
sin, he repents and accepts God's grace. He moves from
wrath to praise.

And God will set limits to the destruction that man can
wreak. He will pull him back from the brink—"the remainder of wrath shalt thou restrain." Witherspoon sees a great
"beauty and majesty appear when the Almighty Ruler turns
the counsels of wicked men into confusion and makes them
militate against themselves." The heart of the New Testament message lies in a crucifixion that turned into victory
against every possible expectation.

In elaborating the message, he counters that miserably
mistaken belief that man is innately good: "all the disorders
in human society and the greatest part of our unhappiness

. . . arise from the envy, malice, covetousness and other lusts of man." "How affecting it is," he soliloquizes, "to think that the lust of dominion should be so violent and universal! that men should so rarely be satisfied with their own possessions and acquisitions or even with the benefit that would arise from mutual service, but should look upon the happiness and tranquility of others as an obstruction to their own!"

In proof that the mind is "more awake to divine truth" in "a season of public judgment," he sweeps the crammed pews and galleries with his solemn gaze and comments, "That curiosity and attention at least are raised in some degree is plain from the unusual throng of this assembly." As Isaiah put it, "When thy judgments are in the earth, the inhabitants of the world will learn righteousness." From duress will come good, as the Hebrews were told by Paul: "No affliction for the present seemeth to be joyous but grievous; nevertheless afterwards it yieldeth the peaceable fruits of righteousness unto them which are exercised thereby"—unless, of course, people behave as did those who surrounded Jeremiah: "Thou hast stricken them, but they have not grieved; thou hast consumed them, but they have refused to receive correction; they have made their faces harder than a rock."

The underlying consolation of Christianity lies, if one can accept it, in eternity. He puts hard questions to his listeners: "Is it of much moment whether you and your children shall be rich or poor, at liberty or in bonds? . . . whether this beautiful country shall increase in fruitfulness from year to year? . . . or the scanty product of the neglected fields shall be eaten up by hungry publicans, while the timid owner trembles at the tax-gatherer's approach? . . . Is your state on earth for a few fleeting years of so much moment? And is it of less moment what shall be your state through endless ages?"

He led his hearers toward a large view of their situation in which they might discern the possibility of reversing their own values. What was most treasured might be unimportant; what seemed to be the worst of evils might be God's instrument for working out his will. John looked his anxious listeners in the eye and said, "It is the duty of every good man to place the most unlimited confidence in divine wisdom and to believe that those measures of providence that are most unintelligible to him are yet planned with the same skill and directed to the same great purpose as others, the reason and tendency of which he can explain in the clearest manner."

Finally, in a heartfelt appeal that must have elicited a quiver of response, he draws their attention to the pressure of time: "My beloved hearers, . . . I beseech you in the most earnest manner to attend to 'the things that belong to your peace, before they are hid from your eyes.' " The present is the safest time, he gravely told them, "since it is wholly uncertain whether any other shall be yours. Those who shall first fall in battle have not many more warnings to receive."

At last he says what they knew he must: "You are all my witnesses, that this is the first time of my introducing any political subject into the pulpit. At this season, however, it is not only lawful but necessary, and I willingly embrace the opportunity of declaring my opinion without any hesitation, that the cause in which America is now in arms, is the cause of justice, of liberty. . . . The confederacy of the colonies has not been the effect of pride, resentment, or sedition." Further, freedom is a condition of attaining goodness. "The knowledge of God and his truths has been chiefly confined to those parts of the earth where some degree of liberty and political justice were to be seen. . . . [In fact] there is not a single instance in history in which civil liberty was lost and religious liberty preserved entire. If therefore we yield up our temporal property, we at the same time deliver the conscience into bondage."

Then, from the so-called firebrand who was burned in effigy and against whom vicious diatribe was written, the congregation hears assurance that he does not consider the king and Parliament to be "barbarian savages. Many of their actions have probably been worse than their intentions. That they should desire unlimited dominion . . . is neither new nor wonderful." After all, they stand to lose a good deal, should the colonies separate. "Would any man who could prevent it give up his estate, person and family? . . . Surely not. This is the true and proper hinge of the controversy between Great Britain and America." A temperate statement from one whose feeling in the matter was so high! He adds a practical observation that the British are so far away that it is hardly to be expected that they could be effective in administering the colonies. If for one year Parliament cannot "conduct their quarrel with propriety . . . how can they give direction and vigor to every development of our civil constitutions, from age to age?"

The sermon runs to thirty-nine pages in print, and the above condenses about half of it. The last part of the sermon turns from theological concept to a miscellany of advices upon a variety of subjects, and it is not much exaggeration to say that it seems as if he had removed his gown, stepped down from the pulpit, and started to talk with the graduating class. His language retains its dignity, but the content bubbles up from a life that has been very much engaged in the world's affairs and lived by a man who observed and judged what went on around him:

Eschew "a furious and angry zeal for . . . contentions of one sect with another." Truly, "there are few surer marks of the reality of religion than when a man feels himself more joined in spirit to a truly holy person of a different denomination than to an irregular liver of his own."

Merely the "form of godliness" achieves nothing. "All those insensible secure sinners, however decent and orderly in their civil deportment, who live to themselves and have their part and portion in this life," are no more likely to avoid sin than "the heaven-daring profligate or grovelling sensualist."

"Pure principles" are a condition for political decision. This phrase means that one does not propose opposition because of "turbulent spirit or a wanton contempt of legal authority; from a blind and factious attachment to particular persons or parties; or from a selfish rapacious disposition, and a desire to turn public confusion to private profit—but from a concern for the interest of your country, and the safety of yourselves and your posterity."

Hypocrisy is familiar enough in those who appear more pious than everyone knows them to be, but it is equally bad to "seem to have less religion than you really have. . . . What a weakness and meanness of spirit for a man to be ashamed in the presence of his fellow sinners to profess that reverence to almighty God which he inwardly feels." This deprives many of an influence they could use, for, in truth, "we contribute constantly, though insensibly, to form each other's character and manners."

Prudence, firmness, and patience are urged, with admonitions not to "judge every measure over again" once a decision is made nor to "intermix little private views . . . or marshall into parties, the merchants against the landholder" nor to let "provincial pride and jealousy [cause you] to speak with contempt of courage, character, manners or even language of particular places." (Had news reached him of how much New Englanders and their ways had irritated Washington?)

God helps those who help themselves he told them—in many more words than that. He adds, "I would neither have you to trust in an arm of flesh nor sit with folded hands and expect miracles should be wrought in your defence. This is a sin which is in Scripture styled tempting God."

"A general profligacy and corruption of manners make a people ripe for destruction." Profanity, that "flagrant enormity," is "one horrendous lack of manners. . . . The horrid sound of cursing and blasphemy . . . cools the ardour of [a Christian's] prayers and abates his confidence and hope in God." Wage war against it—and let the British army revel in its reputation for being champions of blasphemy.

The higher your position the greater your obligation to combat profanity or any evil. Silent example is not enough. "There is a dignity in virtue which is entitled to authority and ought to claim it." Besides, Scripture admonishes you not to hate your brother in your heart but to rebuke him.

Boasting of victory shows a sorry lack of gratitude to God who deserves the credit. "Pardon me, my brethren," he interposes, "for insisting so much on this but I look upon ostentation and confidence to be a sort of outrage upon providence and when it becomes general and infuses itself into the spirit of the people it is a forerunner of destruction." Remember Goliath.

It is impossible not to conclude that a winning aspect of all Witherspoon's sermons lay in his own person and delivery. Witnesses agree that, with a deliberate articulation in that flat voice and heavy Scottish accent, he lacked the obvious attractions of an orator. But, using no notes, he spoke from the depth of his own belief with directness and sincerity to bedrock concerns of humankind. He was a believable person, well known to a great number of people who recognized his ability and integrity.

When the sermon was published in Scotland, scorn from old enemies suggests that they had not read it. A Glasgow editor called John one who had "considerably promoted if not primarily agitated" the whole trouble in the colonies. Another Scot took a swing at him by prefacing a satirical poem with a dedication to "Dr. Silverspoon Preacher of Sedition in America" in whom he saw "political drunkenness." On the contrary, a reviewer of the London edition of 1777 found "more piety than politics" and thought it might well have been "delivered with great acceptance and possibly . . . good effect before any Fast Day audience in the Kingdom."

Close on the heels of the Fast Day sermon, Witherspoon became predominantly a political man. On June

11 he found himself in Burlington as a new member of the provincial congress. That evening, as a matter of course, he opened the session with a prayer. Ashbel Green tells us, "Many of those who took the lead in the arduous struggle which issued in the Independence of our country were . . . men of decided piety; and those of opposite character yielded to their influence, from a regard to popular opinion, which at that time was strongly in favor of religion."

Green was in a position to know. His father was in the congress, and from him he learned of its quality: "Men of distinction felt that the post of honour was the post of danger; and that more than ordinary exposure to a bullet, a bayonet or a halter was not to be coveted nor the risk to be assumed lightly. The whole population felt that they needed, for the management of the great interests at stake, all the wisdom, talent and fidelity, which they could find in the community. Wherever these were found . . . the services of their possessors were demanded, in a manner that could not be refused without loss of reputation. Refusal was considered as evidence either of Toryism or Cowardice."

Elias Boudinot, who would later become president of the Continental Congress, at that time had his reservations. For one, he was dismayed to find three ministers in a gathering at Burlington. "Our clergy have unhappily gone distracted," he wrote, "and will do us more injury than I am afraid they will do us good." After forty years of wrangling with the Church of England on the separation of church and state, he rued that "we are running into the same extreme."

One honorary and three actual graduates from Princeton formed with President Witherspoon the delegation from Somerset County. They were immediately faced by a crucial decision: should they follow the recommendation of the Continental Congress to dissolve the government of the Crown and establish another? Yes! ruled the provincial congress.

In ten days they disposed of Governor William Franklin, sending him prisoner to Hartford, Connecticut, after an angry confrontation before the congress. Witherspoon let himself go in an excited response to Franklin's charge that the congressmen knew little about government. Tradition says the royal governor also cast aspersion on their humble birth, a delicate topic from an illegitimate son—even of so distinguished a parent as Benjamin Franklin. This so enraged John that he poured forth an answer that was partly lost as he lapsed into his native speech. But it was widely reported that he ended with a sentence loaded with sarcasm which he later regretted: "On the whole, Sir, I think Governor Franklin has made a speech every way worthy of his exalted birth and refined education."

The next business was to vote new delegates to the Continental Congress. The count revealed that they had chosen Abraham Clark, a surveyor and high sheriff of Essex County who had been in the first provincial congress; Honest John Hart, a farmer of great good sense; Francis Hopkinson, a Bordentown lawyer who was a musician and versifier and had been director of the Philadelphia Library Company and customs collector at Newcastle, Delaware—rivaling even the versatility of Franklin; Richard Stockton; and John Witherspoon. "These delegates," Green reports, "were instructed 'if they should judge it necessary and expedient,' to join with their associates 'in declaring the United Colonies Independent, promising to support them with the whole force of this Province.'"

It was the twenty-second of June. After a mini-career of eleven days in the provincial congress, John hastened back to Princeton, handed the running of the college over to Prof. Churchill Houston, then set out for Philadelphia on horseback with Richard Stockton and Francis Hopkinson. They made an early start, covering the fifty miles by midafternoon when they rode into the city in a crashing thunderstorm. After finding their way to the statehouse, they discovered the door to the elegant room with its twin fireplaces where Congress was sitting. As John Adams was closing his argument for independence, they walked in.

# 6

## Peripatetic Congressman

### Their Blood is on the Hands of the British.

*—Inscription in Princeton cemetery on students' tombstone*

## 1776–1782

The three rain-wet Jerseymen stepped into a room filled with weary members of the Third Continental Congress. Sitting as a committee of the whole, they had listened to the pros and cons of—at last—a resolution for independence submitted by Virginia's Richard Henry Lee on June 7. John Dickinson of Pennsylvania had delivered the epitome of reasons against it, and John Adams was concluding his points in favor. Adams did not regret the interruption. Three votes for independence had just arrived.

Those who wanted to postpone the decision also welcomed the men—as an excuse for delay. A suggestion was made that the new arrivals should have a recapitulation of the debate to aid their decision. Also, as John recalled later to Ashbel Green, the point was made that "the country at large needed more time for reflection and was not yet ripe for so important a decision." At this the Scottish congressman whose membership was only minutes old made a firm statement that information on the current situation had been available to the new delegates, they had weighed it carefully, and their decision was ready to be recorded. The country too, he said, was "loud in its demand for the proposed declaration and in his judgment it was not only ripe for the measure but in danger of becoming rotten for the want of it."

Witherspoon did account for the changing of two words in the Declaration of Independence. He vociferously objected to reference to "Scotch and foreign mercenaries" among the enemy (although Howe's troops in Boston had indeed included a Highland regiment). "Scotch and" was struck out.

Even though Witherspoon cannot be credited with swaying congressmen in "the nick of time," as an unsubstantiated tradition would have it, his participation in debate was frequent, sensible, and diverse. He employed to advantage his custom of delaying speaking until others had laid out lines of argument. As he confided to Green, he would wait for a moment when he could make a good transition into remarks he had previously written out and fixed well in mind, then rise for what seemed to be an extemporaneous speech.

He was vigorous in expressing his opinions on the Articles of Confederation. Strong for granting one vote to each state, he opposed Benjamin Franklin, who wanted the vote based on taxable population. Franklin asserted that the confederation could hardly last if small states, which paid far less for its support, had equal voice. Witherspoon cited Holland's one-state, one-vote government and the East India Company, where each stockholder had one vote regardless of his number of shares. He opposed as demoralizing the very suggestion that the confederacy might be a weak government. He urged swift formation of a common government to bind the colonies without delaying to search for perfection. He observed that future change was always possible and asked, "Shall we establish nothing good because we know it cannot be eternal?" He suggested, with unaccustomed idealism and surprising prophecy, that the American confederation might be a model for large sections

—whole quadrants perhaps—of the globe to devise "some plan of union to perpetuate security and peace."

During his first half year in Congress, Witherspoon shifted from concepts of government to such particulars as wagons and clothing. His first committee appointment was to procure wagons for the public service. Was it a compassionate clergyman who influenced the committee to urge against seizing property and to favor returning it after use, with avoidance of violence to property or person? As a member of the standing committee on clothing, John eventually set up an émigré weaver from Paisley in Nassau Hall to produce uniforms. By October his appointment to the Committee on Secret Correspondence, later the Foreign Affairs Committee, gave him his most important congressional role. Here lay the duty of procuring foreign aid, an essential determiner of the outcome of the war.

Witherspoon's administrative experience made him appreciate centralized authority. He favored a strong central executive for America's new government and authority for the head of a mission rather than separate reports from each member as some preferred. By this stand he strengthened a mutual regard between himself and Franklin, the acknowledged chief of mission to France.

As the year 1776 rolled on, war took on increasing reality for New Jersey. Early in November, John had his first contact with the enemy: he took four prisoners of war to Princeton, where two of them worked on the Tusculum farm. Throughout the war, he had various assignments with prisoners, British and American. He obtained for them better conditions, or exchanges, and, for a number of imprisoned New Jersey loyalists, releases. Collins opines that "as governor of a body of young but chronic objectors at college," the president was "in some subtle way equipped for settling the very real grievances of older and more genuine captives."

It is fairly amazing that when he brought the prisoners to Princeton, President Witherspoon attended to college business and made his usual announcement of opening for next term. Customary room assignments were issued on November 6. This although Washington was in northern Jersey and, pursued by the British, would very evidently be marching soon down Princeton's main street!

Congressman Witherspoon had conferred with Washington in Newark on ways to replenish thinning American ranks (from eighteen thousand to six thousand) and, returning to Congress in late November, he stopped at the college to do what he must. From an unknown student's diary we have the account: "Our worthy President deeply affected at this solemn scene entered the Hall where the students were collected, and in a very affecting manner informed us of the improbability of continuing there longer in peace; and after giving us several suitable instructions and much good advice very affectionately bade us farewell. Solemnity and distress appeared almost in every countenance. Several students that had come 5 to 600 miles, and just got settled in College, were now obliged under every disadvantage to return with their effects or leave them behind, which several through impossibility of getting a carriage at so confused a time were obliged to do, and lost their all."

In the best of times, horses for a journey had to be reserved months in advance, and at that moment no farmer wanted to part with his mounts. Also competing for horses were legislators of the newly constituted State of New Jersey, who were meeting in Princeton with their new elected governor, William Livingston. They fled to Trenton and then to Burlington, where they soon disbanded.

Students did what they could. The diarist moved to the home of a tutor to continue his studies, but the youth soon enlisted and went off with the army. Two of the young men who remained in Princeton, the Rupert brothers, were buried in Princeton cemetery in early January under a stone with the grim notice, "Their Blood is on the Hands of the British." Another student, captured on his way to Philadelphia, was saved from execution by the intervention of Washington. Yet another was shanghaied by Americans! He ended his journey in the Dutch West Indies, where, as Collins points out, he heard and saw at Saint Eustatius "what was probably the first foreign salute to the American flag."

To Samuel Stanhope Smith, who had married Witherspoon's daughter Ann, John wrote a "very full and particular account" of removing the family from Princeton. This letter is lost, but it is known that he took them to Smith's father's home in Pequa, Pennsylvania, on the Susquehanna about seventy-five miles west of Philadelphia. His wife, Elizabeth (also referred to as Betty), rode in the "chair," a light one-horse carriage, which was driven by a future governor of North Carolina. He was Benjamin Hawkins, a senior from the college. All the belongings that "could be carried upon one team" of four colts driven by John Graham were convoyed by John on his sorrel mare. Sons John and James were already soldiers, and David was with the Smiths in Hampden-Sidney, Virginia. Daughter Frances presumably rode along to Pequa and later joined her brother and sister in Virginia.

Congressman Richard Stockton had just returned from Albany, where he inspected troops and found "a great part of the men barefooted and barelegged," with no shoes or stockings to be bought anywhere. The Stocktons were burying their silver in the garden when Annis remembered documents of potential danger in Whig Hall. By fetching and hiding them, she earned the first feminine membership in the Whig Society. Richard drove his wife and four of the children to a friend's in Monmouth County, where he was seized by Tories in the middle of the next night and hauled into Perth Amboy as a special prize—a signer of the Declaration. The British gave him an agonizing time and a grievous decision: pledge yourself to no further activity against the British or remain in prison. He sadly signed an agreement to become inactive and returned to his family. Wounds to body and spirit healed but slowly.

A little later John Witherspoon heard the dismaying news that a Princeton alumnus, the Reverend John Rosburgh, had been killed in Trenton by Hessians.

Washington and his men whisked through Princeton on December 2. Five days later the British came. They gave the village a miserable three weeks. But in this time, Washington showed the Redcoats what could be done by surprise, vigor, and persistence. After returning across the Delaware from Bucks County in Pennsylvania, he captured Hessian troops at Trenton on Christmas night and, returned to Princeton for the well-known battle near Stony Brook. Alexander Hamilton's artillery, in dislodging British from Nassau Hall, sent at least three balls into it. One with inadvertently appropriate aim beheaded the portrait of King George II in the prayer hall. General Alexander Leslie, comfortably settled in the president's home, left hurriedly. On the table breakfast was ready to be eaten. It was eaten—by hungry Americans.

For nearly two years, until November 1778, Nassau Hall housed soldiers—roistering and destructive ones, wounded and ministering ones. To Dr. Benjamin Rush, writing in Princeton on January 7, 1777, the state of the village was calamitous. "You would think it had been desolated with the plague and earthquake, as well as . . . war; the college and church are heaps of ruin; all the inhabitants have been plundered; the whole of Mr. Stockton's furniture, apparel, and even valuable writings, have been burnt; all his cattle, horses, and hogs, sheep, grain, and forage, have been carried away by them; his losses cannot be less than five thousand pounds." Rush had a special interest in Morven, for, just a year before, Dr. Witherspoon had married him to Julia Stockton, the sixteen-year-old daughter of Richard and Annis. In the meantime, Alfred Hoyt Bill observes, the three gentlemen of the wedding party together had signed the Declaration. Now the health of one of them had been broken by imprisonment, one had fled, and one stood appalled in the midst of the ruined scene.

The prosperous peaceful little town had suffered griev-
ously but a bit less than Rush indicated. Jonathan Dickinson
Sergeant's new house had been burned, but the town itself
had not been put to the torch. Neither the church nor Nassau Hall had collapsed, as his words imply. But windows
were broken, and the interiors of both were devastated.
Horses had been stabled in the church, and pews had been
chopped up for firewood. Woodwork in Nassau Hall had
been torn off and floors ripped up to warm the freezing
soldiers, as much if not more damage done by Americans
than by the British.

In fact, British officers had set a guard on the precious
orrery, reportedly to take it home as a war trophy. It was
known to have been whole when the Americans arrived, and
the inquisitive boyish soldiers put it quite out of kilter; it did
not run again for more than 150 years. The prayer hall
organ, the first organ to accompany Presbyterian singing in
America, had been annihilated except for its case. Other
furniture of the hall had become fuel. Only a few pieces of
scientific equipment were left. The library, with its books
brought from England and carefully added to, was devastated. Some of the books had been used for kindling.

John Witherspoon was as distraught as one would expect
a man to be whose work has been shattered. His fellow
congressman Thomas Nelson, Jr., in a letter to Thomas
Jefferson written before the British had even left Princeton,
reveals that John had heard the desperate news: "Old
Weatherspoon has not escaped their fury. They have burnt
his Library. It grieves him much that he has lost his controversial Tracts. He would lay aside the Cloth to take revenge
of them. I believe he would send them to the Devil if he
could, I am sure I would."

John was less vehement about Tusculum, perhaps because his chief loss there was his animals, more replaceable
than books, and his personal library there was intact, including, actually, the tracts. The big loss, from which we suffer
also, is that his office in Nassau Hall had been ravaged. His

papers were gone, with what personal notes and letters we
shall never know. Richard Stockton too might occupy a
larger place in history had not one wing of Morven been
burned and Stockton's papers destroyed.

Shortly after Witherspoon settled his family and returned to Philadelphia, Congress too took alarm and fled
the oncoming British. John Adams bought two horses and
a brace of pistols for a ride to Baltimore on December 12
where Congress reconvened. There Witherspoon planned
with members of a special committee to invite foreign aid.
These efforts were more successful than attempts to supply
sufficient clothing for the army, a lack of which continued
throughout the war.

The fund-raising committee proposed a "plan to send
commissioners to Vienna, Spain, Prussia, and the Grand
Duchy of Tuscany; to induce France to assist the United
States openly for certain considerations; and to have the
commission to France prepare treaties of commerce and
alliance with Spain and Russia." A Memorial of Facts, written later as John reviewed his congressional service, indicates his strong support for these steps.

Baltimore offered a degree of social gaiety. Adams mentions a dinner party for twelve, including John, at the Lux
mansion. There a portrait of George III still hung—upside
down. When Witherspoon preached, Adams heard "an excellent sermon . . . but I perceive that his Attention to civil
Affairs, has slackened his Memory. It cost him more Pains
than heretofore to recollect his Discourse." Still, he had
found the topic, *Redeeming Time,* well developed, a true compliment from a discriminating mind.

By early January 1777, the American army was hibernat-
ing in Jockey Hollow outside Morristown, and the British
had gone north. It was safe for Congress to continue in
Philadelphia until the next threat arose. John wrote a
strongly worded report on atrocities of the British in New
Jersey, vividly referred to by Thomas Nelson, Jr., in the
letter mentioned above: "There is Scarcely a Virgin to be

found in the part of the Country that they have pass'd thro'
and yet the Jersies will not turn out. Rapes, Rapine, and
Murder are not sufficient to raise the Resentment of these
People."

John opposed the appointment of Thomas Paine as secretary to the Committee on Foreign Affairs. Shortly before
the war Paine had been editor of the *Pennsylvania Magazine*
to which John contributed both money and articles. He
found Paine inconsistent and unreliable, a writer who had
to "quicken his thought with large draughts of rum." Paine
had also edited some of John's work as being "too free."
Paine did receive the appointment; later he was released for
breach of confidence.

Although engrossed in his congressional work, John
never forgot his major commitment, the college. He was not
the only congressman whose life included a counterpoint of
concern with his private affairs. Congressmen were not paid
in the first years. Those without a business or farm operat-
ing in their absence had no income. John needed his presidential salary and no doubt wanted to earn it.

Still, it is rather breathtaking to learn that in March 1777,
with windows still out of Nassau Hall, part of it in use as a
hospital, and its equipment ranging from poor to nil, John
issued a notice for students to return on the usual opening
date, May 10. By July 10 the College of New Jersey actually
did reopen. Trustee Richard Stockton looked into minimal
repairs necessary to retard deterioration of the building.
Boys brought their own textbooks, and credit was given,
after appropriate examination, for work done at home.
Seven young men were even graduated at a private commencement in September, twenty less than the year before.
Classes met in the president's home, and boys lived with
families in town. Gallant Professor Churchill with one tutor
comprised the faculty, and the president visited them when
he could.

The trustees asked John to petition Congress to prevent
further military use of Nassau Hall. It quartered troops until

June 1777, served as a distribution point for supplies, and housed the wounded and prisoners. The petition was granted; troops were barred from the building, but the last patient did not leave until November 1778. Tailors for the New Jersey Brigade remained more than a year after that, and it was 1782 before it was once again only a college.

By May 1777, John was drawn into congressional work in which he showed unexpected aptitude: finance. In raising money for national needs, he and Robert Morris became close associates, and the latter found a loyal supporter in the president. Witherspoon spoke vigorously in Congress against paying army suppliers by commission rather than by contract, of issuing too much paper money, of reneging on interest of government bonds. His grasp of basic economics was respected, and later New Jersey turned to him to aid in its financial problems.

On a quite different level was the matter of how to choose major generals. It was proposed that they be elected by general officers. Witherspoon recalled the year that he let the senior class at Princeton select its own honor men. "So much ill-feeling and confusion resulted" that he reverted to appointing them himself. This experience appealed to congressmen, who voted to do likewise.

In September, Congress was again hurled into flight, this time in dire urgency following Washington's debacle at Chadds Ford on the Brandywine, hardly more than twenty miles from Philadelphia. A few days after the battle, Adams recorded: "The City seems to be asleep, or dead, and the whole State scarce alive. Maryland and Delaware the same. The Prospect is chilling, on every Side. Gloomy, dark, melancholly, and dispiriting. When and where will light spring up?" The next day: "We are yet in Philadelphia, that Mass of Cowardice and Toryism." But that night at 3 A.M. he was awakened and told that the congressmen had gone, a few soon after midnight. Alexander Hamilton had sent a dispatch saying that the enemy could be in the city by morning. Adams and Mr. Merchant rode up the Delaware to

Bristol and breakfasted with a number of their colleagues.

They hurried on to Trenton and dined there with other congressmen, including Witherspoon. Adams describes a "Scaene of Desolation" at General Dickinson's home where Hessians had dug up the greenhouse floor, snapped off his orange, lemon, and lime trees, and broken bottles all around. A woman where he was staying truly observed "that private Property will be plundered, where there is an Army whether of Friends or Enemies."

With Congress scattered and attempting to convene once more in Lancaster, Pennsylvania, Witherspoon foresaw that little business was going to be accomplished for a few days. He returned to Princeton and there on October 4 heard news from another battle—at Germantown. This encounter was heavy with meaning for him.

His son James was killed there. It was thought that one cannonball accounted for the simultaneous deaths of James and General Nash. Twenty-five years old at his death, James had graduated from Princeton in 1770 and then had gone to his father's holding in Vermont at Ryegate. He spent two years as a settler there, building his own house before getting into the conflict as a spy near Saint Johns, Quebec. After returning to Princeton, he joined Washington's army and went with it to his death. Neither of his parents was present when his sister Ann and one of his brothers saw him buried in Germantown. The president was back at his desk in Congress, then meeting in York, Pennsylvania, on October 7.

The most trenchant satire ever produced by John came from this British occupation of Philadelphia. It was not published for more than a century, which is well. It jibes unmercifully at the Reverend Jacob Duché, chaplain of Congress, who had written a piece called *Caspipina's Letters*. Witherspoon's scathing sequel, *Caspipina's Catechism*, demolished the man who is at present nobly portrayed in some of the bicentennial memorials that overlook the Reverend Mr. Duché's rediscovery, on the arrival of the British, of his subconscious loyalties to the Crown. He became a Tory and explained himself in his published letters.

His act released so much adrenalin in Witherspoon that he poured onto paper the most superlative of all his exasperations:

Question. Who is a Turncoat?
Answer. The Rev. Jacob Duché.
Q. What is your Reason for that Opinion?
A. Because the late Chaplain of the Congress has entered with Zeal into the service of Sir Wm. Howe.
Q. Who is a Fool?
A. The Rev. etc.
Q. What is, etc.?
A. Because he attempted to Shew that his Conduct was not absurd and inconsistent. . . .
Q. Who is a Blasphemer?
A. The Rev. etc.
Q. What is, etc.?
A. Because for a long Tract of Time he solemnly called upon Almighty God conscious of the Insincerity of his own Heart. A Citizen & Traitor is to blame, a Soldier & Traitor is a Rogue, a Chaplain & Traitor is a Blasphemer. . . .
Q. Who is an Ass?
A. The Rev. etc.
Q. What is, etc.?
A. Because he set his Name to his Letter. He was a Rogue to conceive it, a Coxcomb to write it, but an Ass to set his Name to it.
Q. How comes it that so many Inconsistencies meet in one Man?
A. I can give no other Account of it but that if God Almighty has given a Man a topsy turvy understanding, no created Power will ever be able to set it right End uppermost.
Q. What was your Opinion of him before?
A. That he was a weak superficial—& his empty Flashes hardly merited Attention.
Q. What is your Opinion of him now?
A. That he is a Wretch without Principle, without Parts, without Prudence, & that by an unexpected Effort he has crept

up from the Ground Floor of Contempt to the first Story of Detestation.

So much more passionate than any other of his writings, the *Catechism* might be seen by a psychologist today as a projection of his grief for James's death and for the whole senseless overwhelming destruction of war.

Already on the standing committees on clothing and foreign affairs, he was now appointed to another, the Board of War. This gave him a front-row seat in the military arena. His first duty here did not add luster to his name. General Burgoyne, after his surrender of Ticonderoga in October, had accused Americans of violating the convention, hence, he claimed, releasing the British from their own obligation to it. In an acid personal characterization of Burgoyne based on hearsay, Witherspoon called the general "a man showy, vain, impetuous, and rash," one to "take advantage of this pretended breech of the convention to wipe off the reproach of his late ignominious surrender." Historians have not supported the indictment delivered by the vehement Witherspoon.

On a committee to respond to overtures for peace delivered by Lord Howe and General Clinton to Washington, John joined in a refusal to negotiate their "half offers." A similar attempt was rebuffed when Prof. Adam Ferguson of Edinburgh and the Earl of Carlisle wanted to present a proposal. Ferguson later wrote to Jupiter Carlyle that only half the population of America "with Johnny Witherspoon at their head" was against the British. He "trembled at the thought," he wrote, "of the cunning and determination of Johnny," of Franklin and Adams and several more of "the most abandoned villains in the world." Witherspoon must have been pleased at the company in which he was named but not deluded into thinking of himself as the leader.

Ferguson's reference to a small group of men keeping the revolt alive reveals a conviction of various foreigners: a junto controlled Congress and would dominate the government once independence was won. France's first minister to America, M. Gérard, had reported on such a political phenomenon in which "a Scotch minister named Wederspun, the only man of his profession in Congress, was the soul of his party; he united in high degree two qualities seemingly opposed, extreme forcefulness of character and the greatest pliability of mind *(souplesse d'esprit)."* In reality, Witherspoon was far from wishing to be "indispensable when capitulation of the British took place," as Gérard charged, and there was in fact no such group.

Other engagements of the year for John were, as always, varied: aiding in the reorganization of the Board of Treasury; more considerations of money and finance; drafts of a response from Congress to M. Gérard's first speech before it, of thanks to Lafayette, of credentials and instructions for Franklin as minister plenipotentiary; designing seals for the Treasury and Navy Departments. He finished the year by representing New Jersey in the ratification of the Articles of Confederation.

The college needed its president, who in turn was eager to get the institution back on its feet. With great reluctance he yielded to pressure to return to Congress in 1779 and did so on condition that he be free to absent himself when duty called in Princeton. During that year his attendance was sporadic.

In March he expressed once more his long-standing conviction that the public should hear the truth whenever possible. He had dissented when Congress wanted to keep secret the contents of papers that the Committee on Foreign Affairs brought forward during the investigation of Silas Deane. John Jay wanted more discretion and complained to Washington that Congress had no more secrecy than a boarding school.

That summer he traveled to Vermont as a member of a committee investigating claims that the states of New Hampshire and New York had made on land known as the New Hampshire Grants. Residents of a part of that land called it "Vermont" and were already functioning as if it were an independent state. This was John's second or third long horseback ride to Vermont. He was gone for six weeks during which he and another of the four-member committee talked with the governors and many inhabitants of the region. In the end the committee disbanded without eliciting congressional action.

Meanwhile, at Princeton he had been engaged in housekeeping. By November of 1778 the usual curriculum was again offered, although four years elapsed before all activities were restored. The influence of inflation could be seen in a petition to the state legislature to change the limit of income that could be held by the college from £2,000 sterling to the value of 30,000 bushels of wheat. The president's salary, however, remained at its pre-inflation figure. Congress granted £7,250 as rent for its wartime use of Nassau Hall. No damages, however, were paid, and the rental money was in depreciated currency worth only 26 to 1. This held repairs to essentials, namely, the roof and the front windows to give the place a less spectral appearance. Account books show that all through that year carpenters and glaziers were paid, and boards, lime, "nails and oyl" were purchased—about £4,000 worth in all.

Somehow recitations were held in the Hall during the winter of 1778–1779. Several students even lived in it but all boarded with families in town. John wrote a report in April 1779 for all concerned to know exactly how the college fared. Well may we wonder that commencement took place, not quite as usual, about the time of the battle of Brandywine. The occupation of Philadelphia a few days after, followed by the defeat at Germantown, all within fifty miles of Nassau Hall, does not seem an ideal ambience for scholarly pursuits; but William Churchill Houston, with occasional visits from the president, kept the college and grammar school going. The next summer when the Battle of Monmouth was fought, even closer to Princeton, there seems to have been no inclination to another flight. It was two years before another military tread was heard—American troops going to fight in the south.

Meanwhile, John wrote in his report that "the Grammar School . . . is in a thriving condition, there being nearly thirty boys in it. . . . Great care is taken to make the scholars accurate in the grammar and syntax and . . . to perfect them in reading, spelling, and pronouncing the English language; a branch of education of the first importance and yet often shamefully neglected."

Commencement that year sharply reduced the ranks of undergraduates: six of the ten enrolled graduated. Notwithstanding, at the trustees' meeting a new professor was added to the faculty, Samuel Stanhope Smith. No reference to Smith as a person omits the word "elegant." He was a man of great style, an orator with all the flourishing eloquence Dr. Witherspoon lacked. He was a handsome and charming person with an excellent mind, administrative ability, and a winning way with students.

Smith had graduated from Princeton the year after the Witherspoons arrived and later read theology with Dr. Witherspoon. He successfully courted the president's daughter Ann and took her to Virginia. There he eventually became the first head of Hampden-Sidney Academy. John surrendered half of his annual salary of £400 and the president's house on campus to lure the Smiths back to Princeton. Smith relieved John of certain administrative duties and taught moral philosophy. John and Elizabeth moved to Tusculum, living there with their daughter Frances, who in 1784 married Dr. David Ramsay of Charleston.

David Witherspoon coincidentally married in North Carolina the widow of General Nash, who had died with James Witherspoon. David at nine had delivered the Latin salutatory for the grammar school the year after his arrival in Princeton and as a freshman in the college won the Latin prize. A year after he graduated from Princeton in 1774 his brother-in-law Samuel Smith found work for him at Hampden-Sidney. In 1777 he entered the army as a lieutenant,

but before the war ended, he was studying law and then
became secretary to the president of the Continental Congress, Mr. Huntington. Practicing law later in the vicinity of
New Bern, North Carolina, he served in the legislature of
that state. Death came to him prematurely at forty-one. He
was buried in the Nash vault, which was destroyed during
the Civil War. Apparently successful, he left property,
slaves, and a son, John Nash Witherspoon. John's career
would have cheered his grandfather: he studied at the University of North Carolina and received two honorary degrees from Princeton—the last a Doctor of Divinity when he
was Moderator of the General Assembly.

David—or his family—took better care than the others of
letters from his illustrious father, for nine survive. No other
letter to any member of his family has emerged. Four were
written to David in 1776, two in English and one each in
Latin and French. They sound like a caring father who is a
minister and would write *Letters on Education:* "Keep pen &
Ink always about you or by you & take Notes of many things
as well as your Expenses. . . . Take particular Care of your
behavior for a Character is soon formed & often easily lost.
. . . I do not know so general or so excellent a Rule for good
Manners as to think concerning others as every good Man
ought to think. If you wish them well in your heart you will
certainly be civil to them in your Behavior." Later, Witherspoon writes that he has been told *"que vous ne vous mêlez
point avec les folies & badinages des jeunes gens"* ("that you don't
get mixed up with the follies and banterings of young
men").

Witherspoon's other surviving child, John, had gone to
France to procure medical supplies in October 1779. True
to the talent of the Witherspoons, John had delivered the
valedictory in Latin at the age of twelve when he graduated
from the grammar school. In college, his sophomore classmates Aaron Burr, Jr., and Henry Lee, Jr., trailed him in the
competition for reading Latin and Greek, but at their commencement in 1773 he, like David, was not even an honors

student. He went on to study medicine, and as a doctor he went to Boston with Washington in 1775, thereafter serving in army hospitals. The year 1781 found him as surgeon on the American privateer *De Graff* when it was captured. After a wretched experience in an English prison, he was eventually extricated by Benjamin Franklin.

At the end of 1779 President Witherspoon was firm in his resolve not to return to Congress. William Churchill Houston replaced him, so the president and his son-in-law ran the college alone. Those two able men had no difficulty in coping with the small complement of students. Pursuit of the war was desultory and far from New Jersey. But it continued, and inflation was still uncontrolled. It was the wrong time to mount a search for funds or students. Witherspoon turned his thoughts to education in general.

A letter by him in the *New Jersey Gazette* is an interesting statement of principles and methods for elementary education, much of it still apposite. It could well be the anguished plea of many a teacher today, were it directed toward students' use of English instead of Latin.

Train students to be accurate in their use of classical language, John begged of teachers. Be sure that they understand syntax. Thorough comprehension of structure is worth many a line of translation. He recommends certain books but adds that, as every schoolboy knows, a good teacher is worth more than any book. Secondly, increase vocabulary by translating English into Latin and using easy books, written to build vocabulary, instead of forcing students through advanced classics. "Boys who say they have read Vergil or Horace who yet cannot speak three sentences in Latin upon the most common subjects" are the despair of the president. Students should read and pronounce Latin correctly, but one should expect from them also accurate English. Finally, master one step before going to the next —and that by easy stages, else all is lost.

The latter part of the letter, for parents, is still pertinent. They are exhorted not to push children, for a boy finds it "more honorable as well as pleasant" to top one class than to be at the bottom of a higher class. If a boy cannot remain for the degree, then let him omit courses not essential to his needs instead of botching a full program. Further, "he should not be called home on trifling occasions or . . . for frivolous pretences." In John's words, it "extinguishes their emulation and often produces a despondent indifference and sloth." When boys insist "that they will study hard to make up the time," what teacher will not smile with John, who says, "but experience tells me that the very reverse is commonly the case"?

We could still truly say that parents tell children that certain things are harmful and expect the college to prohibit them, then "when [the children] return home . . . all those things are done frequently, openly and without reserve. Perhaps," says John, "I shall hereby expose myself to the reproaches of that honourable class of men the Free thinkers of the age; this gives me very little concern."

Another event of the summer was the arrival of a French horseman, the Marquis de Chastellux, riding down the main street and dismounting for a closer look at "an immense building, visible at a considerable distance." His next words would pierce many a son of Nassau: "remarkable only for its size." After approaching the building "by a large square court surrounded with lofty palisade," he dismounted to investigate. Soon joined by the president, who conversed in French, Chastellux "easily perceived that he had acquired his knowledge of the language from reading rather than conversation." The Frenchman, obviously amused, continued in French, "for I saw that he was well pleased to display what he knew of it."

The visitor, an admirer of Washington, asked to see the local scene of battle. A Colonel Moylan was called, and Chastellux passed, as he said, "from Parnassus to the field of Mars. . . . [The two men] were both equally upon their own ground; so that while one was pulling me by the right arm, telling me, Here is the philosophy class; the other was plucking me by the left, to show me where one hundred and eighty English laid down their arms."

By October the president was back in the political arena, now as a state senator. He warmed to his first task, a report to Congress on the situation of New Jersey. He was forceful in picturing the special difficulties of his agricultural state. It had supplied food and forage at every call, and now, Witherspoon pleaded, it was time for other states to do their share. Jersey families were seriously deprived of their own produce.

This was scarcely dispatched when, for a second time, John's service to the state was cut short as he was elected to Congress. He went, although he had recently written to a Scottish friend that he could not afford to be a member of Congress: "None of the delegates are allowed to have any lucrative office whatever, either in their own state or for the United States." In his letters refuting the much-talked-of junto of which he was supposed to be a part, he also revealed a demoralizing condition: "the congress is changing every day"; "this year all the delegates were changed but one." Indifferent attendance of congressmen led to frequent lack of quorum, which ground business to a halt. The very gravity of the situation, however, must have challenged John, who had confidence in himself, with ideas of what should be done. He wanted to speak for his own state, which would need defense when Virginia and New York told Congress that their western boundaries were the Mississippi, if not the Pacific. So Dr. Witherspoon returned to Congress.

Soon after his return to his familiar desk with the green baize cover and silver inkstand in Independence Hall, Witherspoon made a proposal. In January he moved that Congress be empowered to levy and collect taxes on imports and to oversee commerce. States were inconsistent in their import taxes and not at all regular in turning them over to Congress. For some congressmen this proposition gave too much power to the central government. The motion was lost.

As chairman of the committee to seek ways and means of paying for the campaign, John had more power. The committee reported a plan to limit activity of separate states: cease the issue of paper money, pay into the United States Treasury their arrears, turn their bills of credit into the national government, accept definition of state boundaries by the central government, which would then use western lands as a fund of credit. States were also asked to bar formation of any more banks. To us this seems reasonable. In 1781 it immediately evoked protests of infeasibility and injustice. Representatives were accustomed to think of their own states first. They were familiar with the state unit, and beneath an admitted need for central authority lay the fear of the very object of their rebellion: a despotic unresponding head of government supported by its legislators. Not all realized that in fighting a war for six years and negotiating together with foreign countries, the states had already remarkably expressed common consent.

Many congressmen felt the need for concerted action. With some alteration they passed the recommendation of John's committee, which also authorized the superintendent of finance to collect hard money, pay the most pressing debts immediately, and liquidate national debts as soon as possible or fund them as loans if creditors preferred.

The other major concern of Congress in 1781 was its instruction to John Adams in France when he came to bargain at the peace table and to try to win European friends. There Witherspoon was also deeply engaged. His ability to speak French was used in conferring with the French minister, M. La Luzerne; his ability to write was employed in correspondence—a significant function, for if words were ambiguous, it would take two months to answer a question.

The instruction to the commissioners—John Adams had been joined, with Witherspoon's concurrence, by Franklin, Jefferson, Jay, and Henry Laurens—have long been a bone for historians to gnaw upon. Did the French minister to the United States virtually dictate the instructions? Witherspoon was an ardent Francophile, and he was close to M. La Luzerne. Prof. Edward S. Corwin thought that with America's realization of France's utterly essential aid and sympathy it seemed justifiable to "vest France outright with the trusteeship of American interests." With rivers of sweat and torrents of oratory, that is virtually what the committee did. The words were written by Witherspoon, decisively underlined with his own quill pen. The instruction directed Adams only to insist on total independence and to uphold the existing treaty with France. Otherwise, it was "unsafe at this Distance to ty you up by absolute and peremptory Directions." The final admonition was to confer on everything with "ministers of our generous ally the King of France, to *undertake nothing without their Knowledge and Concurrence.*" In the end the commissioners ignored the instruction and used their own judgment.

One odd request came to Congress that year, involving John in a manner disturbing to him. Colonel Morgan—of Prospect-near-Princeton—had become guardian for three sons of Delaware chieftains, who were to be educated in Nassau Hall Grammar School. The Board of War had made this arrangement, and it billed Congress for the Indians' maintenance. Asked to reimburse him, the Board of Treasury countered that President Witherspoon had several years earlier received a "large sum of specie" to cover subsistence of exchanged prisoners; let him draw on that to pay Colonel Morgan. Against John's protest, he was ordered to account for and pay over the monies.

In April of 1781 a production emerged from Witherspoon's pen, curious for its timing if not for its subject. The *Pennsylvania Journal* printed four more *Druid Papers,* a series of essays that John had earlier begun. In these he turned to the language of Americans, still an engaging subject. In fact, H. L. Mencken's massive volume *The American Language* opens with several pages quoted from Witherspoon. Mencken found John fastidious at times, but the president had a fine sample of eighteenth-century language with comment on how it struck an educated ear. He credited "the vulgar in America with speaking much better than the vulgar in Great Britain," but he thought that "persons of higher classes in America have more errors in grammar and vulgarisms than in higher classes of Britain."

John had been struck by Americanisms such as "fellow countryman" (the adjective is superfluous) and "a certain Thomas Benson" (in England "certain" is indefinite, not particular). There were vulgarisms, present too in England: abbreviations like *an't*, *can't*, and *don't*; *know'd* for *knew* and the commonly used *drownded*. *Lays* for *lies*, still ubiquitous, troubled John as did "equally as good" and "He said as how that was his opinion."

A man who said he had "been to Philadelphia" offended Witherspoon's Scottish ear, which would rather hear that he had been *at* or *in* Philadelphia. He preferred persons to walk *into* the house rather than *in*. Strange locutions such as *a spell of sickness* and *a bad spell* might, he thought, derive from sea dialects. Local phrases were seen in the Middle States, where a man will *once in a while get drunk*. John did not fault him for getting drunk, but he preferred it to happen *sometimes*. Pure error can be encountered anywhere: *eminent* for *imminent*, *successfully* for *successively*, and *veracity* for *credibility*, which confused the character of the person with the truth of the story told. Cant phrases are tiringly overworked such as *taken in, helter-skelter, the Devil to pay*, and *his ipse dixit* —"all these taken from printed pieces, some of them by authors not contemptible." Of course he was pained by *a man of accomplished ability*, because there is "an irregular marriage of the adjective to the wrong substantive." This random sampling does small justice to his neatly developed seven categories.

In February of 1782, the House of Commons voted to cease hostilities in America, and in April the Dutch Republic recognized the independence of the United States. The next month John was reelected to serve in Congress until November. In June, with the nationhood confirmed, the statesmen were pressed to face once more the old problems of finance, which led back again to the troubling question of the western lands.

Witherspoon penned a report from the committee on finance, recommending an end to bills of credit from Europe and encouraging prompt payment of interest and duties on imported goods. Another proposal brought Congress into a deep altercation which went on for months and in which John was often a forceful speaker. A potential source of wealth for the nation lay in the sale of land to the west of the states. Several states claimed the Mississippi as their western boundary, but proof was lacking, since early charters were necessarily vague. Witherspoon proposed that since title could not be established by the states, title to all the western lands should be acknowledged to the king, as it already was in existing treaties. In the peace treaty to be drawn, cession of those lands to the United States could then be demanded of the king.

In the midst of passionate claims and counterclaims, an application arrived from the people of Kentucky to be admitted as a new state on the very grounds Witherspoon had enunciated: their soldiers had sworn allegiance to the United States, not to Virginia, then "the charter under which Virginia claimed the country had been dissolved and in consequence the country belonged to the Crown, and that by the Revolution the rights of the Crown devolved upon the United States."

In answer to the quick protests of Virginians, Mr. McKean of Delaware hoped that no one state would presume to give laws to the rest. Dr. Witherspoon rose and delivered his thoughts, preserved in Charles Thomson's minutes of Congress: "One of the gentlemen from Virginia had said that it could not enter into the thoughts of any man that the rights of the Crown devolved on the United States; he supposed this was intended only as a figure of rhetoric, not as an assertion that would be admitted. It certainly could enter into the thoughts of men and had actually entered into his thoughts, and it had entered the thoughts of the petitioners and into the thoughts of the very many sensible men at the beginning of the present controversy." Further, "it would appear a strange whim if a sentiment which occupied and engrossed the minds not only of speculative but of illiterate men and the bulk of the inhabitants of many of the states had not some solid foundation to rest on."

He proceeded through considerations of the powers of Congress, suggesting that the time might come when it might have to "abridge the power of some State and even to divide it into two or more distinct and independent States." He ended by mildly confessing that he could not say whether the people of Kentucky were in Virginia or not, but that "he saw no impropriety in letting the petition remain on the files of congress."

At the end of September, Congress was not in the least in a mood to accept the doctor's point of view. Eventually, after he was no longer a member, it settled the question in a manner that showed it had heard him.

While these considerations were Congress' major concern, John commended to it the wish of a printer in Philadelphia, Robert Aitken, to publish the Holy Bible. Congress approved the printing of the first complete English Bible in the United States, hoping it "would be as advantageous as it was honorable to the printer who was risking his private means in the enterprise." By the time it was printed, Bibles from England had arrived at a far lower price, and poor Aitken lost his shirt.

In November, Witherspoon came to his last act in Congress. He wrote the eighth proclamation since the war began for a day of thanksgiving. By chance it fell on Thursday, November 28, eighty years before Thanksgiving became a national holiday. He called for "praise for great and signal interpositions of Providence" which he enumerated, and one, ironically, was the "instance of divine goodness to these States . . . [in] the harmony of the public councils which is so necessary to the success of the public cause." He serenely overlooked a few episodes in his reference to "the perfect union and good understanding . . . between the United States and their allies." Still, one cannot doubt that when he led his congregation his own thanks were ardent and sincere.

John Witherspoon's career in Congress stands rather like a marble statue, solid material with good lines clearly discernible. Like most statues, it is better from some angles than from others. But color is lacking; details that give life to an oil portrait are almost wholly wanting. Witherspoon himself left no personal comment on Congress, its members and the way they worked, no private opinions of what was going on around him.

What others might have said about him is tantalizing. Why is there not more reference to him in the writings of other congressmen? He was obviously a character, often on center stage. His ability was respected, judging by many calls to serve on committees, often as chairman.

A fair case might be made that Witherspoon was never on quite the same social footing as other congressmen. He was included in social invitations, as Adams tells us; but Adams gives one clue that might account for social distance between Witherspoon and his colleagues. In February 1777, Adams wrote, "I find that I understand the Doctor better since I have heard him so much in Conversation and in the Senate." It was a distraction to hear a man who called himself *Wotherspoon* do what he called *commoonicate!* He may indeed have seemed to be a foreigner.

Even more socially divisive may have been the fact that he was the only clergyman—a Calvinist at that—among many Anglicans and others. (Robert Treat Paine, who signed the Declaration, had studied theology and been a military chaplain. In his mid-twenties he turned to law and was no longer identified with the clergy.) He told Green that he "did not lay aside at any time his ministerial character" and "in sessions of congress or its committees sat in gown

Independence Hall, where the Declaration of Independence was signed

and bands." That surely distinguished him from rich planters and even from Sam Adams, sumptuously clad in gifts from his townsmen who wanted him to hold his own in appearance.

Without family connections in the colonies which others had, he also lacked that easy reference to mutual relatives and family friends which binds many social relationships. His very fame as a preacher and educator may have set him apart in a group in which business, farming, and law were better represented. Or the fact that he knew French, Latin, and Greek. Or that in 1776 he was fifty-three, older than three quarters of his fellow signers and later referred to as "old Weatherspoon."

At least it is true and to a degree baffling that one who was deep in actions and debates of Congress at a crucial time, who was articulate and who showed undoubted ability and good sense on a variety of questions, has by and large been missed by the history books. His attendance alone, more consistent than most, gave his service a valuable continuity from 1776 to 1782—omitting 1780. Green observed that "he sometimes attended without the least intermission during a whole year's term." Yet when most of us think of the Founding Fathers, Witherspoon—if the name comes to mind—has almost no associations for us today.

The very nature of the Continental Congress was something of an *ad hoc* body. With its changing membership and fluctuating power, the Congress simply did not give an ordinary member much chance to be a Founding Father. Its members who distinguished themselves in negotiations in Europe, and those who went on to the Constitutional Convention or who became President of the United States, had different opportunities. It is not surprising, then, that we think first of them rather than of that Scottish-American who in 1782 went back to a village in New Jersey to the institution on which he had worked with splendid effect for seven years.

His son had been killed in the war, his family separated, his college and church ruined, his students dispersed. Yet astride his horse John Witherspoon once again plodded back to Princeton to start its reconstruction.

# 7

## Epitome

> ... the simplicity of a child,
> the humility of a patriarch
> and the dignity of a prince ...
>
> —*Student-secretary's estimate of*
> *his employer, Dr. Witherspoon*

## 1782–1794

Did friends give a farewell dinner at the London Coffee
House when Dr. Witherspoon departed from the Continental Congress for the last time? John Adams, who would have
told us, was at that time writing his diary in France.

Once again Dr. Witherspoon mounted the roan mare for
the familiar ride back to Princeton—through Frankford,
Bristol, across one of the two ferries at Trenton, then those
last miles which the family had first traveled fourteen years
earlier. Between the business of college and Congress, it
was at least the fortieth time he had passed this way. Such
a thought probably never crossed his mind. He was given
neither to statistics nor to retrospection. His single sign of
nostalgia is for his congregation in Paisley. Eighteen years
after leaving it, he was still including his Paisley parish in
family prayers, morning and evening.

John had hoped to spend his latter days in *otio cum digni-
tate*—at ease with leisure. The next ten years, however, were
an epitome of his life—using that word to mean "a part that
represents typically a large and intricate whole." His char-

acteristic activity that did abate somewhat was contention. There was even some of that.

On that November in 1782, enough lay ahead in Princeton to occupy all his thoughts. New Jersey was still suffering the appalling consequences of inflation. Sugar, for example, had increased in cost 1500 percent. The college had benefited from the trustees' foresight in investing funds in United States loan-office certificates whose interest came from France in hard cash. In the spring of 1780, Witherspoon had been able to change $240 of that money for $10,320 of wildly inflated American money. By 1782, Congress was paying interest with its own currency, whose value we still note in the phrase "not worth a continental."

In 1779 "a Jersey Farmer" wrote a letter to the *New Jersey Gazette* of Trenton assigning the cause of inflation to greed, to "a want of virtue or patriotism. I am fully convinced," the farmer wrote, "that we have done ourselves more real damage, by depreciating our money, than the enemy with all their force have been able to do." This passage surely expressed the sentiments of the Jersey farmer who at that moment was making his way to his office in Nassau Hall.

In 1781, Witherspoon wrote a sanguine report on the college, but it was in deep trouble. By 1775 it had capital of nearly £16,000, with its reputation and enrollment constantly rising. But now inflation had devoured nearly 70 percent of those assets. The building and grounds were in a deplorable state, and Congress could not pay for extensive damages done to Nassau Hall by its own soldiers and artillery.

The president's personal situation was no more encouraging. He had observed that he could not afford to be a congressman. Neither could he afford to be a college president! The college owed him nearly £900, and recently he had been paid in low-value paper currency. He had halved that with Dr. Smith, his son-in-law, and generously gave personal help to impecunious students. In one two-year period he kept no less than seven boys in college from his own pocket.

He was to write, "Some who are . . . connoisseurs in economy never can keep their own affairs in tolerable order." He could have meant himself. He had gained a reputation for astuteness in government finance and an equal one for casual handling of his own affairs. He was no bookkeeper, and his trust in others could be misplaced. Besides the episode of the prisoners' fund mentioned above, John signed a government bond for Robert Morris with only an oral agreement on repayment, which later cost his widow an unexpected sum.

An unverified Witherspoon tale adds to the impression that he was naïve in certain negotiations. Returning from Vermont, according to the story, with payment on Ryegate land given in cattle, he fell in with a fellow who offered, for a sum, to relieve him of the role of riding herd. John rode on to Princeton to await his cattle—which never came. It was said that he did not know even the name of the scoundrel.

True or not, these tales reveal a man who trusted his fellows, took no thought of the morrow, and laid up treasure in heaven. He would extend himself vigorously to raise money for his college, but he could not concentrate on a fortune for himself.

His great gift was stirring people with words. He did this again at the Fast Day sermon on April 19 when the village heard the proclamation for peace at the town flagpole, then listened to Dr. Witherspoon in the prayer hall, since the church was still unrepaired. A democracy, he said, is not like a monarchy, which can go through good times and bad times. "A republic . . . must either preserve its virtue or lose its liberty and by some tumultuous revolution either return to its first principles or assume a more unhappy form." Every citizen, "even the meanest and most unconnected," has his influence and sets his example. Not only must the citizen himself opt for the frugal orderly life, but he must choose honest men of high principle to govern.

In May he attended synod and then rode to Vermont to arrange for the sale of his Ryegate property. After giving power of attorney to an agent, he visited in New Haven with his old friend Ezra Stiles, who could well commiserate over current problems of colleges. While the two presidents were exchanging views, a totally unforeseen event transformed Princeton. The little village around Nassau Hall became the nation's capital. Pennsylvania soldiers at Lancaster had marched on Philadelphia, angrily demanding their pay. Congress had hurriedly escaped to Princeton, where citizens packed them into homes and inns, and Samuel Stanhope Smith offered Nassau Hall for their meetings.

When Witherspoon's horse ambled into town in early July, the street was alive with hucksters and visitors as well as congressmen. John Paul Jones, Thomas Paine, and von Steuben were among the throng. European adventurers, land developers, merchants, dancing masters, and fencing instructors passed through town or established themselves. On the fourth of July, students fired cannon and fireworks, and almost every soul in the vicinity gathered to hear them debate "the dangers and advantages of republican government." Ashbel Green, then a senior, expounded so impressively that President Boudinot invited him to his party for Congress that evening at Morven. It was a great gala, and Green got back to his room before curfew at nine o'clock only by the skin of his teeth.

George Washington's arrival to confer on the sort of militia needed for peacetime was the pinnacle of the summer's events. He and Martha and aides stayed at Rockingham, an estate, where an escort of twelve cavalrymen camped in the yard. Witherspoon sent a greeting to the man he so much admired and whose right to full military authority he had defended in Congress. John was no doubt among guests at entertainment for Washington at Morven and at the general's dinner on Rockingham's lawn.

Then President Witherspoon took the center chair at

commencement held in First Church. There a platform and seats had been hastily built to accommodate honored guests and Congress, which adjourned from "the affairs of Empires and the fate of nations to attend on the essays of inexperienced youth," as Ashbel Green wrote. In Green's valedictory, a word of praise for Washington brought a blush to the hero's face.

A British officer, incognito in the audience, put a sinister meaning upon this gathering. His impression, passed on to Lord North, interpreted the morning in First Church as "a farce evidently introductory of the drama which is to follow"—the overthrow of the weak Continental Congress by the junto in which many Europeans persisted in believing. Witherspoon, he thought, was a ringleader; "this political firebrand, who perhaps had not a less share in the Revolution than Washington himself. He poisons the minds of his young Students and through them the Continent."

Washington, always friendly to the college, presented fifty guineas to affirm his support. The college used them to pay Charles Willson Peale for a portrait of the general. It was appropriately placed in the frame where George II's likeness had been blasted during the Battle of Princeton.

The congressional session produced nothing to assure the town a place in the annals of American political history. It almost selected Trenton for a national capital, which led Witherspoon to hope that there would be no permanent capital. The significance of Congress lay, he thought, in the "wisdom of their measures," not in "splendid apartments" for it. He wrote an archetypal description of deliberative bodies when he observed that the question of a permanent residence for the government "always occasioned great altercation; nor was it possible to tell when it was settled; for whenever Congress changed its members, or the members changed their opinions . . . what had been done was undone."

On October 31, two lines of events intersected in the prayer hall as Congress met: a courier arrived with news that a treaty of peace had been signed with Britain; and, its independence thus confirmed, the new nation officially received its first foreign minister, Peter John Van Berckel, Minister Plenipotentiary from Holland. This elating event set off one last round of activities at Morven, Tusculum, and Rockingham. Congress then voted to move to Annapolis.

Under pressure to find money for the college, President Witherspoon, in hope of an appropriation from the State of New Jersey, once again accepted a term in the state assembly.

There he aided in drawing up a law defining conditions for power to grant divorce, sought a way for the state to pay its share of interest on the national debt, and at last made his appeal for aid to his college. By one vote a measure passed for the college to receive during the next two years a fairly haphazard and, as it turned out, insignificant collection through county courts. Although John saw enrollment increase, the financial picture did not glow again in his lifetime.

For a second time his legislative career was cut short, this time by action of the college. The trustees in late October faced the possibility that "the very existence of this benevolent and useful institution is become doubtful, unless . . . relief can be obtained from the friends of virtue & literature, who have not been exposed to such dreadful calamities." These words were part of a letter to Witherspoon and General Joseph Reed, commissioning them to go to Great Britain to solicit funds.

John opposed the move. To petition a country whose men Americans had been shooting at for six years did not, to put it mildly, seem prudent. He also was aware of the hostility toward himself, especially in Scotland. Nothing about such a mission seemed right, but the trustees persisted.

In December, Witherspoon resigned from the assembly, and at Philadelphia he and Reed embarked on the stormy, wintry waters of the North Atlantic. Passengers on the small vessels of those days lived in a proximity almost as close as that of submarine crews today, without being preselected for their amiability. This particular group asked Dr. Witherspoon to propose ground rules for shipboard behavior that might draw them into "a temporary family." His suggestions were "cordially adopted by the whole company, except by one profligate, who declared, in a very impious manner, that he would be governed by no rules, but act just as he should like best." A terrifying storm arose, and the black sheep, in mortal fear, sought the company of the divine. Green, to whom this story had been recounted, set down the ensuing dialogue:

> Profligate: Doctor, this is a most tremendous Gale.
> Dr. W.: It is indeed very dreadful.
> Profligate: I am really afraid we shall all be lost.
> Dr. W.: There seems reason to apprehend that we shall.
> Profligate: The Captain, Doctor, thinks that the ship cannot live.
> Dr. W.: Well, he certainly knows best.
> Profligate: O Dear, Doctor! If we must go down, I hope we shall *all go one way.*
> Dr. W.: There, Sir, you must excuse me—*I hope we shall not.*

The doctor survived, but during the voyage he had suffered an injury to his eye. He did not feel much pain from it, but in London a mote blew into the other eye. Attempting to remove it, he closed the eye and discovered that he could not see at all; the injured eye was blind.

Soon answers came in to letters he mailed from London to sound out friends on prospects and suggestions for his mission. These were overwhelmingly negative. Many expressed amazement at such an undertaking. Others expatiated on the current poverty in Scotland. Even Miss Annie Hogg gently wrote, "You know mankind too well, not to know that prejudices once taken, are not easily removed."

Dr. Witherspoon did see old friends, many of whom were

most cordial and none of whom snubbed him. His successor at Paisley invited him to preach, which he did and had the joy of seeing many of his old parishioners.

One unforeseen and thoroughly gratifying experience came from an Englishman, Brian Bury Collins. He wrote that he had been converted through reading some of John's works. Now a Methodist minister, he pledged himself to do his best for the president's mission. Well connected, he wrote to numerous friends, most of whom he found "restrained from showing their usual kindness by prejudice or fear." He had the satisfaction of a short meeting with John in London, and he did raise £50 or £60, some of which John loaned to a poor Scotswoman who wanted to move to America. Only the enterprise of this man enabled John on his return to New York in September 1784 to report a balance of £5 14s. The trustees, dashed indeed, described themselves in "extreme affliction" over the fiasco.

On top of these failures came one more crushing calamity. On Christmas Day the president had ridden in from Tusculum to preach his Sabbath sermon. His stop at the post office was rewarded by a letter from his son-in-law Dr. David Ramsay in Charleston, who less than a year ago had married Frances Witherspoon, "the delight of her associates and pride of the village." John took the letter to the Smiths' house to read it. Ashbel Green, who was present, describes the next moments. The president read: "Charleston, Dec. 17, 1784. Dear Sir—On the ninth instant, Mrs. Ramsay was safely delivered of a son. . . . May heaven support you while I add, on the 14th of this month, at five o'clock in the morning, she exchanged earth for heaven.

". . . I can with truth and pleasure assure you, that such was the tenor of her life, with the triumphant manner of her death, that I have not a doubt remaining that my loss is her everlasting and inconceivable gain. So strongly am I persuaded of this, that if it were possible by any act of mine to restore her to life, I would not do it."

He wrote of her talk with her minister, her pleasure in

seeing her infant son baptized "under the full conviction that she was soon to die. . . . Though sensible of her approaching dissolution, she never once prayed for life, nor did she wish for death. Her whole desire was to be resigned and to submit to God's will, and to be prepared for every event."

As Dr. Witherspoon read that infinitely sad letter in the presence of his daughter's family, "the tears rolled down his manly cheeks," Green wrote, "but he uttered not a word, till he had read it through. He then wiped away his tears, made a few remarks with composure, mounted his horse, and returned immediately to Tusculum. The day which followed, in place of being one of festivity, became one of deep gloom and mourning, both in the college and the town. Mrs. Ramsay . . . possessed in no inconsiderable degree, the wit and sagacity of her father . . . and like him prudence, good nature and piety."

Frances, known as "Miss Fanny," was given by Green even more kind words. Her death, the seventh child lost of his ten children, sorely diminished the family. Of the surviving offspring, an estrangement had sprung up between young John and his father. After his release from the British prison in 1781, the son returned to Princeton for a year or two, after which hearsay places him in South Carolina. There is no indication that he saw his father again, and rumor has it that he was lost at sea within a year after his father's death. David lived in North Carolina, so only Ann Witherspoon Smith was left nearby. Presumably she and her mother cared for Fanny's little son.

Dr. Witherspoon's response to his daughter's death was characteristically forged into words. He preached sixteen successive sermons on "the doctrine and duty of submission to the will of God," all with the text from Luke 22:42: "Father, if thou be willing, remove this cup from me; nevertheless, not my will, but thine, be done." Ashbel Green heard them all and vouched for their strength and poignancy. He rued his inability to find the manuscript of a single one. "The nature of genuine Christian submission was accurately discriminated and clearly illustrated . . . with much practical application," he recalled. "It is not recollected that the speaker alluded to his own particular interest in the subject more than once . . . then however with great effect; and doubtless the circumstances . . . helped to give impression to all that he said." Each sermon stood on its own as a superior unit, and together they fit into a series of powerful effect.

A providential diversion from grief and worry soon presented itself. Dr. Witherspoon was drawn into one last task: the gathering of forces of the Presbyterian Church into a national organization.

The denomination had grown in numbers and dispersed itself geographically. Presbyterian ministers were scattered up and down the Appalachians and into the frontier regions, but in the whole country there was only one synod, the Synod of New York and Philadelphia. Not only did the far-flung congregations need nearer centers of denominational government and better definition of what was expected of them and of their ministry but the country itself was a subject for mission.

War had brought a decline both to American churches and to personal spirituality. Some outstanding Presbyterians had separated themselves from the church—Charles Thomson, secretary of the Continental Congress and an elder in Philadelphia; Benjamin Rush; and James Wilson, a signer of the Declaration.

Action was needed, for every reason. The Presbyterians in May 1785 proposed to develop a more adequate organization, and John Witherspoon was named to chair a committee to scrutinize church government, Scottish and other, and to lay down general rules. Dr. Witherspoon, as an individual, laid before synod an overture to divide itself into at least three synods and form a General Assembly on the lines of the Scottish church.

During the next three years, the Presbyterians worked

their way into essentially the form of church government that they have today. When the first General Assembly at last met in Philadelphia in May 1789, Dr. Witherspoon was the preacher and served as acting moderator through the election of the first American moderator. From these facts, it is easy to assume that the man who undoubtedly was the best known of the denomination, and in many ways the strongest, led the way in its organization. More than one writer has recorded such a conclusion. But Leonard J. Trinterud, turning dusty pages of ancient archives, has brought out a different picture.

The group working on church organization was no more of one mind than Presbyterians ever were in Scotland. Some did not even want a central government, arguing that the presbytery was the real unit of the church. But at sixty-two, Witherspoon did not feel the spur to action that had inevitably stimulated him in his youth. In September 1786 when the committee of which he was chairman had a special meeting in Philadelphia, he did not appear.

Without him the others developed a book of government and discipline. In 1787 he was dropped from the committee. The plan that, after some days of debate, was accepted in the meeting of 1788 can better be attributed to the steady application of Dr. John Rodgers than to Witherspoon.

The Plan of Government and Confession of Faith with a revision of the Westminster Directory gave the American Presbyterian Church its own character reflecting the revolutionary spirit. Specifically, Dr. Witherspoon had, according to Green, prepared the short preface to the Plan of Government. Trinterud grants the possibility of this and considers it a remarkable piece of work, little modified by the synod.

Generally, however, the doctor's contribution to the newly forming church was impressive. Presbyterians had a small group of well-educated ministers whose effect was constantly felt. No one had a larger personal credit for this education than John Witherspoon. Through these men scattered through the middle and southern colonies, Presbyterians were seen to be foremost in insistence upon religious and civil liberties, in assuming social mission, and in ignoring economic stratification, as well as in vigorously maintaining the integrity of the church as the body of Christ. Witherspoon in his personal life had revealed these values; as a college president he had evoked them from many in his charge. His sermons were a continual exposition of his faith; his curriculum had, for its era, been sound and broad.

Witherspoon's responsibilities in the college had to take precedence over participation in church judicatories. He missed more presbytery meetings than he attended, although he closely followed the synod. It is a puzzle why he absented himself from the critical meeting of a committee that he headed. As Trinterud points out, at that meeting in September 1786 the American Presbyterian Church was organized, although most in the church did not realize it.

Regardless of the still-buried reason for what seems a curious defection, Dr. Witherspoon was sovereign when he preached to the General Assembly from the pulpit of the Second Presbyterian Church that May morning, using the sermon he had first preached in America twenty-one years earlier at Princeton. The text was from I Corinthians 3:7: "So neither he who plants nor he who waters is anything, but only God who gives the growth." The theme must have been humility.

Two years later Witherspoon attended, as an assembly delegate, the General Association of Connecticut for Promotion of Religious Harmony. He would have agreed to the new American revision of the Westminster Confession, which allowed for equality of all Christian denominations. A provision in it for civil magistrates to "protect the church of our common Lord without giving the preference to any denomination of Christian above the rest" revealed that Presbyterians as a group were tuned to accept proposals for religious harmony.

Ashbel Green abruptly informs us that on October 1,

1789, Mrs. Witherspoon died. No detail. Two years older
than her husband, she far outlived the average lifespan of
thirty-six years for women of the time. Green, who was only
twenty-six, displayed no sense of the tragedy of a woman
who lost seven of her ten children and never revisited the
friends and family she left in mid-life. He leaves us one
sentence about her, the only existing estimate of her since
Charles Beatty had written his surprised appreciation in
Paisley. Green said, "She was a woman of distinguished
piety, devoted to the promotion of the usefulness and comfort of her husband, a peculiarly fond and indulgent parent,
amiable in her temper, social in her habits, and beloved by
her friends and acquaintances."

There are no other clear hints about Elizabeth. In a long
poem of quatrains referring not only to "W_____n" but to
"Miss Betty," we have a warmer image of her than we get
from the more formal "Elizabeth." John himself may have
given an oblique tribute to his wife in his *Letters on Marriage*
published before the war and reissued several times later.
"Let others talk of the advantages of beauty, wit and
sprightliness," he wrote, "but after seven years of cohabita-
tion not one of them is to be compared to a good family
management, which is seen at every meal and felt every
hour in the husband's purse." No matter, he thought, if
such a wife does "not appear quite killing to a stranger on
a visit."

For his era he took a large view indeed when he wrote,
"It is of little consequence whether the superiority [of un-
derstanding] be on the side of the man or woman," just so
the command is quite clear. Should others consider the less
wise husband as "henpeckt," he counters: "Should not a
man comply with reason when offered by his wife as well as
anybody else? Or ought he to be against reason because his
wife is for it?" He further observes: "I have known many
women of judgment and prudence who carried it with the
highest respect and decency to weak and capricious hus-
bands: But not many men of distinguished abilities who did

not betray, if not contempt, at least great indifference towards weak or trifling wives."

This sort of thought comes from a man who is either inside a good marriage or longing to be. As the testimonies of Beatty and Green both firmly favor Betty, it seems reasonable to assume that, though likely not "in command," as Green strongly indicates and John's character virtually precludes, she was appreciated by her husband and they enjoyed a good marriage.

The month after Elizabeth was buried in Princeton cemetery, John returned for a third time to the New Jersey Assembly. He was given the key task of setting priorities in the order of business, and he chose for the body to deal with treatment of prisoners, pensions of invalids, public debts, promotion of religion and morality, divorce, paper money, establishment of records of vital statistics, prisoners jailed for debt, and the encouragement of manufacturing. He helped to cope with various of these.

He later chaired a committee concerned with the abolition of slavery in New Jersey. This committee investigated action of other states and reported on current New Jersey law: exportation of slaves forbidden and importation restricted to those belonging to transients and immigrants; manumission encouraged; violent treatment of slaves prohibited. His suggestion to free all slaves when they reached the age of twenty-eight was not acted upon. His opinion that "there was little reason to believe that there would be any slaves at all in America twenty eight years from that time" was optimistic.

Two noteworthy events brightened Witherspoon's later years. In 1786 he published one of his most outstanding articles. Atypical in subject, his *Essay on Money* resulted when even opponents urged him to record his comments to Congress on this topic. In rapid succession the essay was printed in Philadelphia, Charleston, and New York, and was twice reprinted. Of all his works, this was the only one in print in 1974. It remains a simple, lucid introduction to the concept of money. As a sample, his analogy for inflation is a full can, half water and half oil, into which water is poured as oil runs off. In a similar way, he notes, increasing paper money leads to less gold, since the paper and gold together "exactly represent your whole commodity." The commodity increases only when production increases; multiplying paper money, only a symbol, adds nothing real. He goes on to predict exactly what did happen.

Now and again the *Essay* has won favorable notice, as in the middle of the nineteenth century from Joseph Henry. In 1944, President Harold W. Dodds of Princeton spoke appreciatively of how Witherspoon "endangered his popularity for a time" with his "earnest pleas for thrift and honest credit." The economist Prof. Frank A. Fetter called the *Essay* "most remarkable for its grasp of the subject. It equals if it does not excel . . . anything on monetary theory before the Ricardian era."

A few years later Witherspoon's writing career tapered to a close with an unsigned address "To the Reader" replacing the dedication of Bibles to King James. Republican America no longer wanted to recognize a monarch.

The other event was his remarriage at sixty-eight to the widow of former student Dr. Armstrong Dill. Ann Marshall Dill was twenty-four and, as Green wrote, "rendered his second marriage the occasion of much observation and remark, but when his mind was made up and satisfied, few men lived who were less moved by popular opinion or gossip."

The strength of his resolve is all the more remarkable when we find that his suit had already been rejected by one lady. Annis Stockton, handsome and animated in her mid-fifties, was courted by John a year or so after Elizabeth's death. She and her children looked upon him as far too old to be taken seriously as a suitor and apparently spoke rather freely about it. A friend of Annis wrote from New Rochelle with a jocular reference to "the venerable Adonis. Has he yet thought it expedient to propose himself? I find the re-

port travels far and wide." This lady penned a verse on
Cupid's power:

> This little God of Love is a roguish elf:
> He makes old age look foolish as himself.
> 　　'Gainst sixty-two—
> 　　Oh, luckless lot—
> 　　His bow he drew
> 　　And true he shot
> Twang—went the string
> Whiz—flew the dart
> 　　On a *gray* goose quill
> 　　To an old man's heart.

Dr. Witherspoon well knew the reaction his young bride
would occasion. Proof that it was high in his consciousness
lies in his response to the friend in Trenton with whom he
breakfasted on the way to his wedding. This time he drove
with four horses drawing his chaise, a few of which were
brought in from the field. As he took leave of the friend,
who knew his destination, the man looked at the horses and
said in a jesting manner, "Doctor, you do not seem to be
well matched." The doctor mistook his meaning and answered brusquely, "I neither give advice, nor do I take
any!"

Green called on the newlyweds and found the bride
plainer than he had been led to believe. As for a woman's
looks, John had made up his mind about that. In the *Letters
on Marriage* he commented that any man can be carried away
by a beautiful woman, and the poets who write about them
are "directly contrary to what should be the design of every
moral writer." Beauty, he remarked, does not "atone in the
least for any bad quality." In fact, it "aggravates faults because it seems to have held out a false signal," whereas
"almost any other advantage that a woman has will make up
for some shortcoming."

Several students went out to Tusculum, to see the bride,
no doubt, but also commissioned by schoolmates to peti-

tion for a holiday to honor the marriage. The president expansively granted three holidays, which so elated the students that they ended the unexpected vacation with a cannon shot on the front campus signaling the lighting of six hundred candles. These "burned for an hour, while an orchestra in the belfry entertained the crowd with appropriate selections," thereby providing an unusually fine social note for the *United States Gazette.*

If not prospering, the college remained on an even keel. With climbing enrollment, the college deficit was only £11 by 1787. The trustees called a professor of mathematics, the first person since Witherspoon to fill a chair for which he had specific training. By 1789 the books were in the black by £1.

Unfortunately the chart did not slope steadily upward. Records back to 1766 were inspected. Conflicting claims showed that Witherspoon owed the college and that the college owed Witherspoon. An investigating committee disclaimed any derogatory implication of the president and "cheerfully reported that these enquiries are answered to their entire satisfaction and . . . there is no foundation whatever for any impeachment or suspicion of the president's integrity." What can one think but that there had been rumors less cheerful than the committee's report? The final accounting showed the president to be owing £186 9s. 8d. "which could be easily and satisfactorily explained," perhaps by a provision in John's will that contributions given him to help impecunious students be returned to the college, up to £200.

Samuel Stanhope Smith's position in the college became more prominent as Dr. Witherspoon grew older. Student life was relatively free from excursions and alarms. The young men celebrated the founding of the French Republic with a public dinner at a tavern, and the fall of the Bastille led to a great ball. By that era a dancing master in the village had a number of clients among students. The good old stern days were gone.

Drama also became a college activity, but the president did not approve. He favored debating, where his experience in polemics made a great and lasting effect. The debating societies, Cliosophic and American Whig, rivaled each other intensely and often, constituting a unique character of the college. Almost every student was fired to action in them, and some alumni reached distinguished heights in the use of language and persuasion. Philip Freneau and Hugh Brackenridge are recently credited with the first American novel. In 1770 these two from Whig wrote a satire directed against Tory classmates in Clio which, in 1975, has been called "an important piece of intellectual history." Other society leaders were William Paterson, later governor of New Jersey and subsequently a supreme court justice, and James Madison.

Madison, that student of Witherspoon who rose highest, to an unsurpassed role in the creation of the Constitution and to the Presidency, deserves special mention. Madison lingered at Princeton for graduate work after his commencement in 1771. He read theology and ethics with Witherspoon and surely had the opportunity to imbibe ideas that may later have affected his judgment of the needs of a people in the nation's government.

Prof. James Smylie has traced the manner in which Witherspoon's Calvinism emerges in the American Constitution through Madison's influence: man's innate depravity, of which Presbyterians are keenly aware, must be checked by counteracting forces; self-interest of individuals necessitates that government should limit it for the good of the whole; faction—"impulse or passion or interest adverse to the rights of other citizens or to the permanent and aggregate interest of the community," as Madison described it—separates men into groups; faction is inevitable, not removable by education, social engineering, or religion; and a workable government must recognize this. Then that government must be shaped so that one set of interests will keep other sets of interest from dominating. Checks and balances are required. Dr. Smylie thus connects Madison's political philosophy, with its import for us all, to instruction he received from the man he affectionately referred to as "the old Doctor."

In the last three years of his life Dr. Witherspoon was blind. His one good eye, damaged in a fall from his horse in Vermont, had gradually ceased to function. He consented to try surgery in Philadelphia. Green spent the eve of the operation with Dr. Witherspoon, who personally had no hope of improvement. "The temper of mind which he manifested was truly christian," Green wrote. "It had pleased God to grant him the use of his eyes for a long time; and if it was the divine will that he should never more have the use of them in this world, it would give him little concern." He told Green that he felt fortunate to have lost his sight rather than his hearing, which would have meant the loss of "the cheering influence of the human voice, the pleasure and advantage of free conversation." Unfortunately, the operation did fail.

A great consolation in his blindness was his third cousin, John Ramsay Witherspoon, who arrived at Princeton in November 1792 as a sophomore. He became the doctor's secretary. Green, writing his memorial of Witherspoon in 1840 in his own old age, added valuable pages to his work by posting questions to the younger man.

Every third Saturday evening, young John would read to Witherspoon one of his sermons. The next day, led into the pulpit, Witherspoon would deliver the sermon almost verbatim, and more fluently than the secretary could read it from a script which, though it looked well, was often illegible even to the writer. The president, when reading a lecture, had disarmingly admitted to classes, "Well, well, I suppose I knew what it was when I wrote it, but I cannot tell what it is now." The young cousin was appreciative of the "familiar, instructive and paternal" conversation of the old man, even though the Saturday sermon-reading rather ruined the youth's holiday.

In May of 1794 the doctor attended the General Assembly, more as an honor than to work, and a few months later he began to suffer from dropsy. This did not prevent one last public appearance in September, when he conducted commencement exercises "with his usual propriety and dignity." He also conducted the trustees' and faculty meetings soon after.

His "descent into the grave," the secretary tells us, "was gradual and comparatively easy, free from any severe pain, and contemplated by himself with the calmness of a philosopher and the cheering hope of a christian." Fortunately he was not bedridden and his mind was clear. Another student wrote to his father the events of the evening of November 15:

> They had sent for Doctor Smith that Night and when he came they read the news of the last paper they had, but Doctor Witherspoon was still desirous to send for the last paper. They sent for it but before the boy had arrived with the paper, they found him dead sitting on his chair.

Witherspoon was buried in "Presidents' Row" beside his predecessors. The next May, Dr. Rodgers preached a commemorative sermon in the Princeton church, and seven years later the trustees raised enough money for the stone slab that bears a long inscription in Latin written by Samuel Stanhope Smith. Especially striking are the words "affable, charming and agreeable in private conversation, and a man of extraordinary skill in the public affairs of the church. . . . He shone for a long time among the brightest lights both of education and of the Church."

John Witherspoon D.D., L.L.D., son of the above; President of Princeton College New Jersey U.S.A. Member of Congress and signer of the Declaration of Independence 1776; was born in the manse here 5th Feb. 1723, and died in his adopted country 15th Nov. 1794. An upholder of Liberty, his life now takes on a new significance 1918.

Plaque affixed to parents' gravestone in 1918

# Epilogue

What did John Witherspoon leave to his survivors? An estate. Printed works. A record of political service. A life as a churchman. A career as an educator.

His goods and chattels are quickly mentioned. In bequeathing £50 to each of three children from his first marriage, he reminds them that he had already given them a good education and cash gifts. To three grandsons, all namesakes, he left £200 each. Half the remainder and all his real and personal property went to his wife, Ann, "not doubting she will be particularly careful of the education of any child or children whom I shall leave behind me."

He and Ann had two daughters, Frances, ten months old at the time the will was drawn in September 1793, and Mary Ann, born before the year was out. Frances proved to be an ill-starred name in the family, for two months later this daughter also died. To Mary Ann went the other half of her father's liquid assets, and into her possession eventually went a handsome grandfather clock upon whose silver face "Paisley" is incised. Was it a farewell gift to a minister leaving for a distant land? It now stands in the foyer of the Presbyterian Historical Society, purchased in recent years from descendants of Mary Ann and the "very respectable clergyman" she married, James S. Woods of Lewistown, Pennsylvania.

The inventory signed by Ann included a library worth $640 and ranged through equipment of farm and home, such as two yokes of oxen, 14 cattle, 10 horses, 24 sheep, 18 Windsor chairs (total value: $8), down to one old sleigh at $1.33, and an easy chair, which must have been well sat in, appraised at $1. The superb clock was valued at $36. Two twenty-eight-year-old slaves were "supposed to be worth $200." The balance at the bottom of figures none too clearly annotated is $2,835.68.

Witherspoon's printed works have been sampled here at some length. After his death, two editions of his collected *Works* were published: in four volumes in Philadelphia, in nine volumes in Scotland. Twenty-one years after the president's death, even among many Scots who would have valued little the books of Johnnie Witherspoon, the Edinburgh publisher thought a reprint worthwhile.

Sermons comprise more than half his works. Resounding statements of faith and exhortation, they expose no new theology. A straightforward Calvinist, Witherspoon's Common Sense philosophy was at vigorous odds with the Scottish rationalism which became deistic; it was likewise incompatible with the American idealism of Berkeley and Edwards. Though clear and orderly with arresting messages, the prolix sermons rarely contain pithy, memorable lines. They were probably better heard than read.

The essays—on marriage, education, eloquence, language, and a variety of other topics—are more appealing today, in their comment on human nature and their practical proposals. Along with some quaintness, many observations are *à propos*. The satires and the unique *Essay on Money* are most readable among works whose style can seem inordinately heavy.

In politics Witherspoon was a willing public servant—in committees of correspondence, provincial congress, Continental Congress, and state assembly. His practical good sense was often cogently expressed; occasionally his judgments were obviously wide of the mark. No one questions, however, his conspicuous, unswerving commitment for independence. His eloquence undoubtedly strengthened the resolve in many of his new countrymen. The bodies of government in which he served, facing problem after problem with no precedent, did not offer the best opportunity to make historical characters of their members. In spite of his years of faithful service, commonly our association of Witherspoon with the Founding Fathers stops with the fact that he signed the Declaration of Independence.

Witherspoon's conception of himself was, first and foremost, as a churchman and minister. In Scotland for two decades he was a church leader, attacking patronage and urging return to basics of Scripture rather than following Moderates into fields that seemed more aesthetic than theological.

A large congregation found him to be a caring pastor as well as a stirring leader. He was always a preacher and for many years a pastor to students and to the congregation of the First Presbyterian Church in Princeton. John Witherspoon was not a leader of the American church in the sense of formulating policy and persuading men to it. In fact, he wielded a passive influence in the role attributed to him of healing the breach between the Old Side and New Side Presbyterians. He appears to have assumed the conflict to be at an end and acted accordingly. His European doctorate, his reputation, and his competence satisfied the Old Side. His consistent Christian orthodoxy and passionate evangelism betrayed so much more than mere intellectual commitment that the New Side could receive him even without a "conversion" experience.

On arrival in the colonies, he served the single synod in various ways, but demands of the college and of national politics soon absorbed his energy. When the Presbyterians formed a national organization after the war, Witherspoon's role may have been less than tradition has given him. In spite of absence at crucial committee meetings, drafts of documents in his handwriting indicate his weight in policy decisions, and his selection as preacher and presiding officer of the first General Assembly leaves no doubt as to his preeminence.

As an educator, both administrator and teacher, he left his most lasting and far-reaching mark. He trained ministers, as he was commissioned to do, but he made the College of New Jersey more than a seminary. No scientist himself, he yet promoted "natural science" and mathematics. His encouragement of debate and oratory stimulated students to arrive at reasoned decisions and to work out answers to political questions. His own participation in government, with its real and great risks, excited students. He stimulated his charges to commit themselves, and he gave them tools for clear expression, written and spoken.

Sheer numbers reveal something of the effect of his college: of the 478 graduates during his presidency 114 became ministers; 13 were state governors; 3 were supreme court judges; 20 were United States senators, 33 were United States representatives; Aaron Burr, Jr., became Vice-President, and James Madison became President. Throughout the Middle and Southern States men went from Princeton bearing, in one form or another, the quality that Witherspoon had described to the Jamaicans as a "wish [not] to live for themselves alone, but . . . [to] apply their talents to the service of the public good of mankind."

The very character of the president was an important part of the education available at the College of New Jersey.

Witherspoon's belief that "truth is in order to goodness" merged his aims as a teacher with those as a pastor: to learn, and to live as a caring and moral person. Both were equally important. He knew that men can "become too much engrossed with human learning and think themselves such great scholars that they are too proud to be Christians." However, "piety without learning is but little profitable and learning without piety is pernicious to others and ruinous to its possessor."

A touching example of a student's appreciation of the president is found in John Ramsay Witherspoon's impression at the age of twenty of Dr. Witherspoon at his life's end: "He had in his manner, the simplicity of a child, the humility of a patriarch and the dignity of a prince; in one moment he was full of humour and wit, in another serious and contemplative—In short he was one of the most interesting and excellent men I have ever seen."

# Note on Sources

Most references come from *The Reverend John Witherspoon,* by Ashbel Green, edited by Henry L. Savage with an illuminating introduction; *President Witherspoon,* by Varnum Lansing Collins; *John Witherspoon Comes to America,* by L. H. Butterfield; and Witherspoon's own *Works.*

For background I have consulted Thomas Jefferson Wertenbaker's *Princeton 1746–1896* and his chapter on Witherspoon in *Eighteen from Princeton,* edited by Willard Thorp; *Diary and Autobiography of John Adams,* edited by L. H. Butterfield; *The Papers of Thomas Jefferson,* edited by Julian P. Boyd; *Letters of Members of the Continental Congress,* edited by Edmund C. Burnett; Edmund S. Morgan's *The Birth of the Republic;* and Alfred Hoyt Bill's small books: *New Jersey and the Revolutionary War, The Campaign of Princeton, 1776–1777,* and *A House Called Morven.*

Material on Presbyterians derives from *The First Presbyterian Church of Princeton,* edited by Arthur S. Link; I. Woodbridge Riley's *American Thought;* Leonard J. Trinterud's *The Forming of an American Tradition;* and Lefferts Loetscher's *Brief History of the Presbyterians.*

Articles and speeches on specific topics have been consulted, such as Gary Nash's . . . *and Distinguished Guests,* a
pamphlet on Congress' months in Princeton; *Madison and
Witherspoon: Theological Roots of American Political Thought,* by
James H. Smylie; Harold W. Dodds's Newcomen Address,
*John Witherspoon;* Moses Coit Tyler's *President Witherspoon in
the American Revolution;* and the funeral sermon on Witherspoon by the Reverend John Rodgers.